D0761818

REFLECTING *the* DIVINE IMAGE

Christian Ethics
in Wesleyan Perspective

H. Ray Dunning

InterVarsity Press
Downers Grove, Illinois

InterVarsity Press
P.O. Box 1400, Downers Grove, IL 60515
World Wide Web: www.ivpress.com
E-mail: mail@ivpress.com

InterVarsity Press® is the book-publishing division of InterVarsity Christian Fellowship/USA®, a student movement active on campus at hundreds of universities, colleges and schools of nursing in the United States of America, and a member movement of the International Fellowship of Evangelical Students. For information about local and regional activities, write Public Relations Dept., InterVarsity Christian Fellowship/USA, 6400 Schroeder Rd., P.O. Box 7895, Madison, WI 53707-7895.

Cover illustration: Roberta Polfus

ISBN 0-8308-1545-7

Printed in the United States of America ♻

Library of Congress Cataloging-in-Publication Data

Dunning, H. Ray, 1926-
    Reflecting the divine image : a Wesleyan view of Christian ethics
/ H. Ray Dunning.
        p.   cm.
    Includes bibliographical references.
    ISBN 0-8308-1545-7 (alk. paper)
    1. Christian ethics—Wesleyan authors.   2. Image of God.
I. Title.
BJ1251.D85   1998
241'.047—dc21   *97-45119*
                                                                                         CIP

20	19	18	17	16	15	14	13	12	11	10	9	8	7	6	5	4	3	2	1
15	14	13	12	11	10	09	08	07	06	05	04	03	02	01	00	99	98		

Preface

My religious roots are in the Holiness movement, which, historically, arose out of the spiritual awakening that initially occurred in England under the ministry of John and Charles Wesley. This awakening flourished in America during the nineteenth century, resulting in the formation of several "holiness" denominations. The representatives of that movement who were instrumental in my family's becoming Christians and joining the church were quite legalistic, and the standards of conduct they preached were very restrictive so far as outward behavior was concerned. Since I had no religious background prior to that time—I was a high-school sophomore—I naturally fell in with this mindset. While I continue to appreciate the emphasis on the disciplined life today, I began to detect problems very early on with this approach to Christian living. My concerns were intensified by inconsistencies observed in the lives of several who were the most vocal spokesmen for this way of thought.

This situation eventually led me through a long search for an authentic Christian ethic. As I pursued my academic preparation for ministry, I began to become aware of pristine Wesleyan theology and recognized that it had some significant differences from the theology that I had learned under that rubric. This awareness led to a deep-seated belief that authentic Wesleyan theology offered a perspective that was theologically and biblically sound. I found John Wesley's own perspective to be extremely helpful and more consistent with the "whole tenor of Scripture," as he put it, than other perspectives I was aware of. The result was that I became a fully convinced Wesleyan, and my theological commitment became a major factor in my quest for ethical understanding.

My thirst for understanding as well as for an adequate preparation for ministry led to my pursuit of a graduate degree with a major emphasis in theology and a minor in philosophical ethics. My professors encouraged me to do something that would make a contribution to my own tradition, and the topic of my dissertation eventually emerged—an analytical study of the ethical history of my own denomination. As I moved into the field of higher education I had the privilege of teaching ethics for over thirty years. During those years I continued to formulate and reformulate my understanding of what an adequate Christian ethic should entail.

The most satisfying conclusion came while I was writing a systematic theology for my denomination, in which I pulled together many aspects of the Christian faith and saw the orderliness of Wesleyan theology. I came to understand more clearly than ever how important it is to anchor Christian ethics in theology.

The culmination of this pilgrimage, through many twists and turns, is this brief book. It reflects what I believe to be an interpretation of Christian ethics firmly grounded in Wesleyan theology and faithful to the Bible, understood holistically and theologically.

My intention is to be true to the Wesleyan spirit, which aims to speak "plain truth to plain people," putting profound ideas in a clearly stated and, when possible, simple form, not stating simplistic ideas that distort the truth. As Wesley himself pursued this self-appointed goal he did not shy away from technical theological language, since he knew that an adequate understanding of any discipline must include the basic vocabulary of that discipline. In like fashion I have made no attempt to avoid technical ethical terminology, but rather to present it in such a way that the careful reader will be able to incorporate it into his or her own vocabulary and read (as well as use) it with understanding. At the same time, it is my hope that the ideas discussed here will be well articulated and thought out so that they can make a contribution to the seasoned student's understanding of the Wesleyan perspective.

PART I

FOUNDATIONS

One

FACTORS THAT AFFECT MORAL SERIOUSNESS

Contemporary society presents a strange appearance that can best be described as moral schizophrenia. On the one hand there is a widespread snubbing of traditional ethical values such as chastity, honesty, modesty, sobriety and marital fidelity in favor of uninhibited hedonism. On the other hand there is an expectation of near perfection for elected leaders and other public figures. In addition, for the past two decades or so there has been an explosion of interest in ethical issues, particularly professional ethics. There are organizations and institutes and multitudes of books and articles dealing with medical ethics, business ethics, environmental ethics, engineering ethics, criminal-justice ethics and so on. As a professor of ethics I have been amazed at the exponential growth of textbooks dealing with these subjects.

What is one to make of all this? Perhaps it simply reflects the subconscious realization that authentic human existence must have an ethical element, as well as the conscious unwillingness to resist indulging one's lower nature. Over twenty-five years ago William Barclay described the general ethos.

Thirty years ago no one ever really questioned the Christian ethic.

Thirty years ago no one ever doubted that divorce was disgraceful; that illegitimate babies were a disaster; that chastity was a good thing; that an honest day's work was part of the duty of any respectable and responsible man; that honesty ought to be part of life. But today, for the first time in history, the whole Christian ethic is under attack.[1]

The intervening years have not improved the situation. If anything, it has worsened.

The general loss of a moral consensus in contemporary society can be attributed to many causes. One factor may be that the truth of ethical moral guidelines, unlike scientific theories, cannot be proven through empirical verification. Perhaps even more influential is the burgeoning pluralism that has eroded the "Christian consensus" of society in general, even in the more conservative groups.

Unfortunately the hedonistic tendency of contemporary society has too often influenced the church. Standards of behavior that have traditionally characterized Christian lifestyles are not as readily apparent among churched people as was once the case.

Toward an Adequate View of Grace

Furthermore, the view of grace that has been dominant in much contemporary evangelical theology has opened the door to the possibility of antinomianism. It would be unfair to say that this fosters immoral behavior; however, there have been some extreme expressions of this idea—that faith alone is necessary for salvation—that offer no safeguards against unmitigated sinning by so-called Christians, for, the theory goes, once one has been "saved" there is nothing that can sever that relationship. And in some quarters there seems to be a celebration of the corruption of "sinning saints."

The emphasis on grace that has been articulated by some influential spokesmen for this so-called grace awakening is not unbiblical, but it presents only one aspect of a multifaceted truth, resulting in an imbalance. The emphasis on this aspect of grace stems from the Protestant Reformation and is solidly based on biblical teaching. In fact it was the "discovery" of this meaning of grace that was the catalyst for Luther's controversy with the Roman Catholic Church. God's love *is* unconditional in that it does not require ethical righteousness on humankind's part as a basis for acceptance. His love emphasizes that we continue in a right relationship with him on the basis of grace, not our own merit. Luther's view of grace being "God's attitude" is orthodox because it is biblical. It is comforting to know, as Luther put it in his characteristic fashion, that "God saves sinners." John Wesley proclaims precisely the same truth in his sermon on "Justification by Faith": "Who are they that are justified? And the Apostle [Paul] tells us expressly, the ungodly; . . . the ungodly of every kind and degree; and none but the ungodly. . . . For it is not a saint but a sinner that is forgiven, and under the notion of a sinner."[2]

A problem can arise from this emphasis on grace when it implies that God deals with sin but leaves the sinner as is. This is reflected in Luther's famous formula *simul justus et peccator.* The believer is at the same time justified and a sinner. A reading of Luther's commentary on Galatians will demonstrate the antinomian tendencies of this teaching.[3] When reading these passages one can hardly doubt the judgment of John Wesley:

> Many who have spoken and written admirably well concerning justification, had no clear conception, nay, were totally ignorant, of the doctrine of sanctification. Who has wrote [sic] more ably than Martin Luther on justification by faith alone? And who was more ignorant of the doctrine of sanctification, or more confused in his conceptions of it?[4]

A more contemporary expression of this same imbalance maintains

> that justification is the sovereign act of God whereby He declares righteous the believing sinner—while he is still in a sinning state. . . . God credited divine righteousness to [Abraham's] account. This occurred even though Abraham was still in a sinning state. But never again would the man have to worry about where he stood before God. He was, *once and for all,* declared righteous.[5]

But a more sound understanding of grace balances *grace as attitude,* or "unmerited favor," and *grace as transformation.* While the latter meaning was dominant in medieval Roman Catholic piety, it was conceptualized in an impersonal fashion that radically perverted authentic biblical teaching. It made transformation the basis of acceptance. The genius of Wesleyan theology is its consistent retaining of a *via media,* or middle way. Its view of grace is a signal example of this trait. Randy L. Maddox, in the most carefully nuanced analysis of Wesley's own theology to date, has demonstrated that this *via media* is the key to understanding Wesley's distinctive emphasis and seeks to capture it in the title of his book, *Responsible Grace.*[6]

Wesley explicitly recognized these two meanings of grace in Scripture in his sermon "The Witness of Our Own Spirit."

> By "the grace of God" is sometimes to be understood that free love, that unmerited mercy, by which I a sinner, through the merits of Christ, am now reconciled to God. But in this place [2 Cor 1:12] it rather means that power of God the Holy Ghost, which "worketh in us both to will and to do of his good pleasure." As soon as ever the grace of God in the former sense, his pardoning love, is manifested in our souls, the grace of God in the latter sense, the power of his Spirit, takes place therein.[7]

Holding to this biblical relation of the two aspects of grace, Wesleyan theology avoids a distorted concept of either justification or sanctification but keeps both in focus. As John Wesley himself pointed out in his sermon "On God's Vineyard,"

> It is, then, a great blessing given to this people that as they do not think or speak of justification so as to supersede sanctification, so neither do they think or speak of sanctification so as to supersede justification. They take care to keep each in its own place, laying equal stress on one and the other. They know God has joined these together and it is not for man to put them asunder: Therefore they maintain, with equal zeal and diligence, the doctrine of free, full, present justification, on the one

hand, and of entire sanctification both of heart and life, on the other; being as tenacious of inward holiness as any Mystic, and of outward, as any Pharisee.[8]

Albert Outler, dean of Wesley scholars until his death, consistently affirmed this same balanced relation as distinctive of Wesley's contribution to the Christian tradition. He spoke often of Wesley's persistent holding together of "faith alone" and "holy living" and his resisting all polarizations toward one or the other.[9]

Sadly, many of Wesley's followers have not maintained the same delicate balance. Many who have opted to emphasize his teaching on sanctification have tended toward legalism as a result of failing to teach it within the context of "faith alone." But the upshot of authentic Wesleyan theology is that it provides a theological context that makes possible an understanding of the Christian life that avoids both legalism and antinomianism.

Personal Ethics

A balanced relationship provides a barrier to another perversion of Christian ethics—a preoccupation with personal holiness to a degree that results in withdrawing from a redemptive involvement in the world. This led to monasticism in the medieval church, and among many Protestant groups it has led to a refusal to be involved in the affairs of the world, such as politics, either for fear of being defiled or because there seems to be no possibility of unambiguous Christian action in these areas of worldly life. But if the holy life is seen within the context of grace and faith, while recognizing the impossibility of a perfectly Christian solution to most political, economic or social issues and that a measure of compromise is essential to participating in the public process, there remains the accepting grace of God.

From the other end of the theological spectrum, those with "liberal" tendencies tend to speak disparagingly of personal ethics as puritanical, thus restrictive and ultimately irrelevant. This approach is usually preoccupied with a social ethic that takes the form of political activism. While this is an important emphasis, it too fails to emphasize personal moral virtue adequately and does not ground its emphases in a balanced theological context. As we will see later on in this study, Wesleyan theology provides such a theological grounding without ignoring personal virtue.

The liberal critique frequently speaks negatively about the conservative Christian's emphasis on soteriology, and some even go so far as to reject the importance of the new birth.[10] This critique is often accompanied by the lament about the failure of the Christian ethic to effect significant transformation either in the church or in the world. But it becomes apparent that this failure could be the result of articulating a Christian ideal that is divorced from the transformation necessary to take that ideal seriously.

Mainline Christian theology has for many years sensed the importance of returning to the idea of sanctification, or the ethical dimension of the Christian life.[11] While it is true that contemporary theology shows considerable fragmentation and preoccupation with many other issues, a review of the catalogs of religious publishers will show that Christian ethics is still a live issue. Much of this interest is directed toward specific problems, so there definitely remains a need for theological grounding.

Authentic Christian faith entails a call to discipleship that involves an inescapable ethical aspect, and Wesleyan theology provides a vision of the Christian faith that provides a solid foundation for developing a Christian ethic that is not one-sided. The questions discussed in this book concern the nature and content of this element of Christian discipleship, as well as guidelines for a Christian lifestyle that will be relevant for the present as well as for the future.

Two

THE NEED FOR A
THEOLOGICAL ETHIC

W hile it is important to recognize the ethical aspect of Christian discipleship, it is equally important to have adequate guidance in living out the ethical Christian life. A number of inadequate proposals have been suggested.

Some suggest that we don't need rules or a system of ethics. All we must do is follow the guidance of the Holy Spirit. While this sounds pious enough and is not to be gainsaid, something more is needed, as experience will verify. There is too much danger of confusing the Spirit's guidance with mere subjectivity. It has happened too frequently to be insignificant. John Stuart Mill was certainly correct when he said, "We need a doctrine of ethics, carefully followed out, to *interpret* to us the will of God."[1]

Closely related to this proposal is another that is often heard and espoused: we should let our conscience be our guide. This too only appears to be a good piece of advice. Its danger lies in the reality that one's conscience is not always a safe guide. What the conscience approves or condemns is influenced by what has been communicated to it. In other words, the content of conscience is learned. As Oswald Chambers once correctly observed, we cannot identify conscience as the voice of God, since, if that were the case, it would be the same in everyone.[2] The diverse standards of right and wrong dictated by the conscience certainly invalidate its being the voice of God. Conscience, to be a safe guide, must be informed by sound ethical understanding. The question is, what is the source of this understanding?

In Wesleyan thought conscience is a theological category. Wesley insisted that it is not to be considered a *natural* trait but the result of prevenient grace. By this he means that the form of conscience is the activity of grace, whereas the content of conscience is learned. He would fully concur with Charles Gore, bishop of Oxford (1911-1919), who said that "man's first duty is not to follow his conscience, but to enlighten his conscience."[3]

The distinction between the form and content of conscience can be compared with Immanuel Kant's revolutionary analysis of epistemology. As he put it, "Form without content is empty, content without form is blind." The content of knowledge is derived from experience, whereas the form or structure is derived from the categories of the mind and imposed on the "sensible manifold."[4] Likewise the recognition of something's being right or wrong is brought *to* experience not by a natural faculty, but through the universal activity of prevenient grace. But whatever is considered right and wrong comes from experience. Thus the specific content may vary from culture to culture and even from person to person, depending on how diverse one's experiences are. This is why it is so crucial to inform conscience with Christian content.

One of the more popular suggestions in "folk" Christianity is that since the Bible is the inspired Word of God, it would be sufficient to consult Scripture for ethical guidance. While it is true that the Bible is the authoritative basis for the Christian faith and life, its specific ethical directives are generally found in a particular setting, often addressed to a culturally conditioned situation. What one must do in many of these cases is penetrate behind the literal instruction to the principle that informs it. The complexity and diversity of the settings for these Scriptures make them extremely confusing at times. This is especially true when injunction and practice do not coincide, as is often the case in the Old Testament. For instance, how does one reconcile the monogamous implications of the creation story with the polygamy of some of the greatest Old Testament saints? Christopher Wright argues that much of what appears to be polygamy on the part of most Old Testament men is really monogamy along with one or more concubines.[5] Yet the principle of monogamy is still violated, perhaps even in a more unacceptable way since it involves keeping a mistress.

Or how do we reconcile the apparent commands of God to wipe out whole peoples with the commandment to not kill, or with the love ethic of Jesus? Or what about a seeming contradiction of a theological principle by a specific directive, as with Paul's instruction to the Corinthian church in 1 Corinthians 14:33-35: "As in all the congregations of the saints, women should remain silent in the churches. They are not allowed to speak, but must be in submission, as the Law says. If they want to inquire about something, they should ask their own husbands at home; for it is disgraceful for a woman to speak in the church"? This is in tension with Paul's statement of the implications of the work of Christ in Galatians 3:28: "There is neither Jew nor Greek, slave nor free, male nor female, for you are all one in Christ Jesus."

These simple illustrations merely open the door to much more serious questions about how the Bible should be used as a source of ethical wisdom. The bottom line is the question of a proper use or method of interpreting Scripture. Robert Bruce McLaren calls attention to the consternation many Christians experience when they realize that the Bible has been "quoted to justify slavery, to bless the profit motive, and to exclude racial minorities from equal participation in society and even in worship."[6]

And yet McLaren himself quotes proof texts from widely disparate sections of Scripture to illustrate, for instance, "seemingly contradictory claims" about human nature, passages that appear to be in conflict with the normative teaching of Scripture. He pays no attention to the context as an explanation for such statements. For instance, he cites Psalm 49:11-12 as a statement of the belief that death is the final parameter to a person's existence. He gives no thought to the fact that this is an Old Testament text spoken from a pre-Christian perspective and should be balanced with 2 Timothy 1:10. McLaren also quotes Ecclesiastes with no apparent recognition that it expresses the meaninglessness of life when seen from an exclusively empirical point of view or in terms of a cyclical view of history.[7]

It is important when using Scripture to identify normative unifying principles that can be applied to diverse situations and settings totally foreign to the biblical world. When this is done one has already identified the raw materials of an ethical theory. But we must beware of using biblical characters as comprehensive models for ethical behavior. Only Jesus can serve as such an ethical model; all others, even the best, must be critically evaluated. They may or may not embody the moral ideals of normative biblical faith.

Exploring the thesis that biblical narrative has ethical relevance by design, Waldemar Janzen has implicitly exposed the clue to identifying the ethical significance of "character stories" in particular—even questionable—situations. He points out that these must be interpreted in the light of the larger story. This means taking into account the theological context in which these stories are set. For instance, he argues that in the case of Phinehas (Num 25) the ethical relevance of Phinehas's action is not to be found in his spear-wielding but in his priestly zeal for the holiness of God. Or in the case of David's sparing of Saul (1 Sam 24:15)—exceptional because he didn't show this kind of reluctance to kill his enemies on other occasions—Janzen notes, "It is clear that our story reaches back and extends forward. It is shaped theologically and contributes to further theologically significant events."[8]

These important proposals demonstrate one way in which the Bible is used as a source of ethical guidance, and they point directly to the thesis we are exploring in this chapter. It is the theological principle that defines the normative ethical behavior of the people of God.

We can thus see the appropriateness of using the Old Testament as a resource for Christian ethical insight, a conviction influenced by John Bright[9] and put simply: The authoritative element in Scripture is the theological aspect. There are no nontheological texts, therefore the whole of Scripture is authoritative for the Christian in terms of its theological content.[10] The implication of this for the Old Testament is likewise quite simple. While literal words or actions may be irrelevant historically and culturally to our contemporary situation, or when the matter involves something superseded by the work of Jesus Christ (such as the dietary laws or the spearing of a couple engaged in illicit sexual activity), the theology that informs those directives remains normative for the New Testament Christian and may be applied to contemporary issues.

This way of reading Scripture is distinctively Wesleyan. Wesley recognized that proof texting could result in a support for virtually any position, but that when individual texts were placed in the larger context of the whole tenor of Scripture they could be more adequately understood. What Wesley meant by "the whole tenor of Scripture" is essentially what we speak of today as biblical theology. Hence, on this understanding, the basic hermeneutical discipline is biblical theology. This structure provides the context for particular segments of the Bible.

The Need for a Theological Ethic

All of this highlights the necessity for a theologically based ethic, that is, one that grows out of and is informed by a comprehensive theological vision. Otherwise ethics can be only an addendum, having no organic connection to the Christian faith. The Wesleyan vision is peculiarly fitted to provide such a theological underpinning. It is true that this tradition has put special emphasis on the doctrine of sanctification, but while not all of Wesley's successors have maintained the balanced view of Wesley himself, he recognized sanctification to be a thoroughgoing ethical concept. Furthermore, a careful exegesis of the New Testament passages explicitly dealing with sanctification (especially the Epistles) will reveal that the vocabulary used is ethical in nature. Hence an authentic Wesleyan and biblical perspective of sanctification will have a peculiar interest in the ethical question.

There are a number of other doctrines that have ethical implications that will be skewed if not properly apprehended. Such doctrines include original sin; the atonement; the church; theological anthropology; justification, especially in its relation to sanctification; and others. I will give a brief overview of two of these that are important for understanding the difference between Wesleyan theology and the views dominant in contemporary evangelicalism. Others will emerge in the development of the specifically ethical sections of this work. It is important to understand that when we speak of Wesleyan theology, we are not referring exclusively to the views of John Wesley as an historical phenomenon. As mentioned earlier, the status of biblical studies in Wesley's time as well as the theological context in which he worked, coupled with Albert Outler's characterization of him as a "folk theologian" who did not develop a systematic theology as such, means that Wesley did not explore all doctrinal themes in full consistency with his central commitments. So to be true to the Wesleyan spirit one must follow those central commitments to their logical conclusions, even if they result in a doctrine that would differ from, even contradict, some of Wesley's own theological comments.

Relation of Justification and Sanctification

One major doctrinal issue on which we have already briefly touched is the relation between justification and sanctification, or "faith alone" and "holy living." Recent biblical studies have illuminated this relation that has long been debated by Christian theologians and has even been a point of division between various Christian traditions. The issue has usually been cast in terms of the relation and significance of *imputed* and *imparted* righteousness. Wesley himself struggled with this issue and failed to find a satisfactory answer.[11] However, he did have unerring insight into the problems involved with each and refused to fall victim to the pitfalls so readily present. Fortunately for us, biblical scholarship has moved beyond the eighteenth century, and we are the recipients of the insight gained, which enables us to transcend this debate with a biblically based understanding that solidly supports the Wesleyan perspective.

The clue to this development is found in the word *righteousness*, which is the root of the concept of justification and which has multiple meanings. Albert Outler is certainly correct in noting that "the ruling metaphor of classical Protestant soteriology has always been the courtroom, together with a cluster of forensic concepts about a human offender arraigned before the divine judge who must, if justice is not to be mocked, convict and condemn the offender."[12]

This is partly true because the Western mentality has always tended to be legalistic in its understanding, and much dominant evangelical theology has been informed by the legal minds of lawyers (such as Tertullian and Calvin). So justification was thought of in terms of ethical righteousness as the basis on which one was accepted into right relation with God and which must be made available for salvation to be possible.

In the Roman Catholic version, a person's ethical righteousness must be in place before justification can occur. This means that in the order of salvation, sanctification must precede justification, which led to the doctrine of purgatory as a necessary prelude to entering heaven when the process of sanctification was incomplete in this life. While this righteousness was initially seen as a gift of God,[13] in time it came to be seen in terms of merit that was acquired either by good works or from someone else's surplus merit. It was this view that became the bone of contention between Martin Luther and the Roman Church when his own experience of this type of soteriology left him frustrated and hopeless of ever being saved.

Out of the agony of his own existential experience, which led providentially to an intensive study of Scripture, Luther discovered another biblical meaning of *righteousness:* God's attitude of mercy extended to those who were incapable of helping themselves. With this insight the Reformation was born. Luther came to see that the "righteousness of God" in Romans referred to the nature of God, not a requirement imposed on humanity, and that this righteousness was essentially equivalent to grace as "unmerited favor."[14]

However, Luther never abandoned the presupposition indigenous to Western theology that ethical righteousness was the basis of humankind's acceptance by God. Thus he arrived at the position that human beings are saved on the basis of an "alien righteousness," one that is "imputed" to the believer, who remains ethically unrighteous because he or she cannot perfectly fulfill the law.

Wesley vigorously resisted both the Catholic and the classical Protestant interpretations. He condemned the Catholic view as confusing justification and sanctification since justification is "not the being made actually just and righteous," even though this may be "the immediate fruit of justification." His strongest reaction, however, was to the concept of imputed righteousness, since justification does not imply "that God is deceived in those whom he justifies; that he thinks them to be what, in fact, they are not." As to the "alien righteousness," he pointed out that God "can no more . . . confound me with Christ, than with David or Abraham."[15]

The closest Wesley came to a definition of justification was his statement that its "plain scriptural" meaning is "pardon, the forgiveness of sins."[16] But when he attempted to adjudicate between imputed and imparted righteousness in his sermon "The Lord Our Righteousness," he bounced back and forth without ever finding a satisfactory solution.

Contemporary biblical studies has shown us a further, perhaps unsuspected, meaning of *righteousness* that can best be termed "relational righteousness." This opens the door to a solution to the long-debated problem of the meaning of justification. In principle, a person is righteous if he or she conforms to the requirements of the relation within which he or she stands. And these requirements are not necessarily—or exclusively—ethical. In discussing righteousness in the psalms, Bernhard Anderson says, "In facing this question we should divest ourselves of notions of righteousness that we have inherited from our culture, largely under Greek and Roman influence. Normally we assume that a 'righteous' person is one who conforms to some legal or moral standard. Such person is held to be righteous according to the law." But the righteousness ascribed to Abraham in Genesis 15:1-6 is different. "The righteousness accounted to him was *being in right relationship* with God, as shown by his trust in God's promise even when there was no evidence to support it—none but the myriads of stars in the sky!"[17]

Thus the requirements of the divine-human relation are faith on humanity's part and faithfulness on God's part, and each is righteous if these conditions are kept. The believer is really justified by faith, and God is righteous when he stands by his promises to accept all who come to him in faith.

With this understanding, the whole centuries-long debate about imputed versus imparted righteousness becomes a moot point since the issue at stake hangs on the presupposition of ethical righteousness as the ground of justification. With the presupposition swept away, the debate becomes pointless. This eliminates the possibility of confusing justification (a relative change) with sanctification (a real change) and reversing the proper order of salvation. It also avoids the legalism that ensues.

The Work of Christ

Closely related to this discussion and a logical corollary of it is the method of interpreting the work of Christ that is dominant in much evangelical theology: a version of the satisfaction theory of the atonement. It too is based on the concept of merit that stems from Tertullian and his influence on Western theology and is brought to culmination by Anselm. While it entails a subbiblical concept of the divine nature, for our purposes here we will discuss how it renders problematic the doctrine of holy living. Swedish theologian Gustaf Aulén highlights this terminal weakness.

> If God can be represented as willing to accept a satisfaction for sins committed, it appears to follow necessarily that the dilemma of laxity or satisfaction does not adequately express God's enmity against sin. The doctrine provides for the remission of the punishment due to sins, but not for the taking away of the sin itself.[18]

No version of the satisfaction theory provides any logical grounds for asserting the necessity of holiness of heart and life. An authentic view of the atonement must provide for both faith alone and holy living, and a fully developed Wesleyan interpretation that looks at Scripture theologically will do this. This will occur when Scripture is viewed holistically and when, in typical Wesleyan fashion, there is a *via media* between Western views of the atonement, which tend to focus exclusively on the death of Christ, and Eastern views, which emphasize the Incarnation. Each is susceptible to one-sidedness, but a holistic view of the work of Christ will include both the Incarnation and the cross in a full-orbed vision of the atoning work of Christ and thus provide for both faith alone and holy living in terms of ethical transformation. This is precisely what John Wesley did, even though he did not develop these insights into an atonement theory.[19]

With these theological observations as a foundation, we are now ready to look at specifically ethical matters, beginning with some important distinctions and concepts necessary for developing a theological ethic.

Three

IMPORTANT CONCEPTS
FOR ETHICAL REFLECTION

Everyone has some concept of right and wrong, no matter how distorted it may be by societal norms. These ideas come from any number of sources, but if one is to speak or think intelligently about the ethical aspect of life, a certain level of knowledge about ethical concepts and distinctions is important.

Ethics—Rules or Principles

Many people think of ethics as a collection of rules by which to order one's conduct. Ethical teachers refer to this way of ordering life as "casuistry." One shortcoming of this approach is that specific rules can seldom be sufficiently comprehensive to cover all situations. This limitation opens the door to the possibility of legalism on the one hand and loose living on the other. Actually, these are but two sides of the same coin.

Ethics by rules of thumb can result in a censorious spirit on the part of those who keep the letter of the law toward those who may deviate from it in any measure or degree. The reported conflicts between Jesus and the Pharisees in the New Testament are excellent examples of this perversion. Furthermore, a legalistic identification of the rules as defining the parameters of ethical behavior can lead to license for any behavior not specifically addressed by the rules. Jesus condemns the Pharisees for precisely this perversion (see Mt 5:20; 12:1-14).

Another negative consequence of casuistry is the near inevitable feeling that the rules absolutely define right and wrong. This makes it difficult to adjust to changing situations in which the circumstances make a rule no longer meaningful. It is natural to conclude that if a certain matter was once wrong, it must always be wrong. This attitude can lead either to an outmoded sense of appropriate behavior or to a wholesale rejection of any ethical guidelines.

The truth is that all children and many adults function at the level of casuistry. All of us unavoidably experience this stage of moral development, but the maturation process should ideally lead us to a higher level of moral functioning.

Morals and Ethics

This leads to the first important distinction that must be made for meaningful ethical reflection: distinguishing between *morals* and *ethics*. While both terms stem from words that simply describe ("morals" derives from *mores* and "ethics" from *ethos*), this book is concerned with more than describing how people behave; we want to look at how they *ought* to behave. Hence, many ethical teachers reserve the term *morals* for the descriptive function and use *ethics* in a normative way. *Morals* describes what we do (or avoid doing), whereas *ethics* refers to *why* we do (or not do) certain things. *Ethics* in this distinction refers to a rationale or set of principles that dictate morals and may be applied to any and all situations. Even more radical, a person's moral behavior may change while his or her ethics remains the same as the "absolute." This truth is illustrated in the New Testament.

In Acts 16:3 Luke tells about the circumcision of Timothy, which was approved, if not actually performed, by Paul. By contrast, in Galatians 2 Paul speaks of Titus's not being required to submit to this rite. In fact,

Paul refused to allow it. Why the difference? Circumcision was a hotly debated point in the early church. The point at issue had to do with the basis of salvation. Could one be a Christian without becoming a Jew first, that is, without submitting to the sign of the covenant (circumcision)? Put more abstractly, it was faith versus works. In the case of Timothy the issue was not whether or not he could be saved without this rite, but it was a matter of simply not offending the Jews. The issue of salvation by faith alone was not at stake. But with Titus the demand was based on the presupposition that he could not be saved without being circumcised, and thus Paul refused. To have submitted in this case would have been to compromise the gospel of grace. In Timothy's case it was an action to avoid a stumbling block and to become a basis for fellowship. The decisive issue was theological, which in different sets of circumstances dictated exactly opposite behaviors. The ethic remained the same, but the morals were different.

There is a similar pattern in connection with one of John Wesley's rules for his Methodist societies. The traditional Judeo-Christian ethic condemned charging rent on money, or usury—charging interest on money loaned, as we say today. So in an early version of Wesley's rules this restriction was imposed. But during Wesley's lifetime the economic situation changed and the realm of business began to build on a more "capitalistic" basis, which entailed using money to make money, or charging interest on loans. Thus in a later version of Wesley's rules the prohibition against usury was changed to a prohibition against charging an exorbitant amount of interest. The principle was unchanged, but the application was adjusted to the situation.

This does not suggest that rules have no value. This would be a situation ethic that really provides no objective moral guidance. Properly understood, rules are statements that codify the collective conscience of the church relating to specific issues. In this regard they have great significance as shorthand ways of summarizing a lengthy ethical reflection. However, they should always be subject to occasional rereflection.

What we are after is not the abandonment of rules but a Christian ethic, a theological principle or set of principles that will guide a truly Christian lifestyle. If we can find what we are after, we will identify an ethic that is transcultural in nature.

Importance of an Ethical Principle

If an ethical principle cannot be established, people are susceptible to all different sorts of influences in determining right and wrong. If there is no transcendent principle, there is no safeguard against the standards of contemporary culture shaping the ethical consciousness of the Christian or the church. Paul warns against this in Romans 12:2: "Do not let the world around you squeeze you into its own mold" (Phillips).

Langdon Gilkey, in a book published in the early sixties provocatively titled *How the Church Can Minister to the World Without Losing Itself,* incisively explored the various forms of church life in terms of the holy, that is, that which is beyond contamination by secular society. Along with several other analysts, Gilkey demonstrates that the denominational form of American church life is particularly susceptible to the encroachments of culture. In a church setting where people attend voluntarily, the pulpit is vulnerable to the pressures of the culture through its members' opinions. It must maintain its population without offending anyone, and only with difficulty can it exercise a prophetic ministry. This situation becomes critical in an ethos that is anti-authoritarian and resists concrete ethical guidance from the minister. The result may be silence from the pulpit on distinctively Christian ethical issues, going only so far as encouraging its congregants to be nice, socially acceptable people.

This disturbing possibility raises another issue. Even if we are able to articulate a normative ethical principle in the light of which moral decisions can be made, it will have relevance only to the person who chooses to accept it. We may rant and rave about duty or loudly proclaim the matter of authority, but ultimately all is pointless apart from an existential decision on the part of the moral agent to submit to that authority, even if it is the authority of God.[1]

Eighteenth-century philosopher David Hume demonstrated beyond any possibility of refutation that apart from physical or psychological coercion (in which case the ethical question is irrelevant) we *always* do what we want to do. In cases where tremendous inward struggle occurs, even though the outcome appears to be contrary to one's normal appetites or inclinations, a stronger desire has taken control. Ultimately, despite the struggle, we still do what we want. As Hume correctly argued, moral behavior is always based on a desire to perform in such a fashion.[2] The implication is that apart from a personal embracing of the theological principle for living out Christian ethics, no amount of exposition or exhortation will make any difference.

This is in agreement with the uniquely Wesleyan approach to holiness of heart and life (ethics). In his "Plain Account of Christian Perfection," Wesley addresses the question "In what manner should we preach sanctification?" He responds, "Scarce at all to those who are not pressing forward, to those who are, always by way of promise; always drawing, rather than driving."[3]

This approach is consistent only with a teleological understanding of the Christian life, since if it were deontological in nature, duty should be proclaimed to the indolent.[4] This raises an anomaly in Wesley's thought, since he seems at times to allow for the legitimacy of two levels of Christian life. One follows the low road and the other the high road. We are left to wonder if this is due to the influence of one of the early church documents known as the *Didache,* or *Teaching of the Twelve Apostles,* which makes the same allowance. Yet this is a minor chord in the Wesleyan symphony and is irrelevant to our purpose in this study.

Philosophical Versus Theological Ethics

From the beginning of recorded human thought people have been seeking to identify normative standards for proper behavior. Almost all philosophers, major and minor, have given some attention to the ethical question.

Truly great philosophers like Plato and Aristotle, Thomas Aquinas and Immanuel Kant, along with numerous others, have explored the issue intensely and extensively.

The difficulty faced by such thinkers is finding a point of reference that will provide a lodestar, a benchmark in the light of which they can make normative pronouncements concerning right and wrong. Without such a point of reference they are adrift in a sea of relativism. However, consistent with the limitations of human reason, philosophers must find their courts of ethical appeal within the limits of this world. That is, if he or she appeals to God as authority, the discussion becomes theological rather than strictly philosophical.

Those philosophers who have taken ethics with profound seriousness have usually made an appeal to human nature. That is, their understanding of human nature provides them with the benchmark. Ethical behavior, they argue, is consonant with becoming an authentic person or consistently manifesting the distinctive character of human personhood. Conversely, unethical behavior is a violation of one's essential nature as a person.

Philosophers who do not take this approach have normally opted bravely for relativism, or even exulted in the fact that humans are autonomous, that is, self-determining so far as ethical values are concerned.[5] This is the direction that much ethical theorizing has taken in recent years and no doubt is one source of the moral confusion that seems to characterize our time.

Theological ethics, on the other hand, properly grounds its ethical ideal in God and includes a person's relation to him as an essential element in the ethical life. If this approach is not taken, there is ultimately a significant weakening of moral consciousness. As Russian novelist Fyodor Dostoevsky said in experimenting with a nonreligious estimate of man, "Since there is no God, everything is permitted."[6]

This book seeks to look at what the ethical life should be in the context of acknowledging the sovereignty and authority of the God and Father of

Jesus Christ for human life. This does not mean that we will not make an appeal to human nature as a source of ethical insight, since that is an essential component in theology. Neither does it mean that philosophical ethics has no value for our consideration. In fact, philosophical ethical theories may provide us with the form or possible forms into which we may pour the content of theological ethics.

Types of Ethical Theory

Another distinction that is fundamental to the central thesis of this book is between two types of ethical theory. One type understands the difference between appropriate and inappropriate behavior in terms of the goal to be achieved. This is commonly referred to as the "ethic of good" and speaks about a highest good *(summum bonum)* that gives moral quality to specific moral deeds. This approach may be nontechnically called an ethic of aspiration. It has a means-end structure. That is to say, I follow a certain lifestyle because I am committed to achieving a specific end, and this lifestyle is best suited to reaching that desired end.

This approach is often criticized by identifying it in terms of the formula "the end justifies the means," thus describing a way of justifying immoral behavior. It is not the formula that is questionable but the perversion of it. If I use any means, no matter how destructive to other persons or nature, for that matter, to achieve my own selfish goals, it is clearly immoral. But clear thinking will reveal that first, self-gratification is not a worthy end, even though some hedonistic versions of ethical thought may support it; and second, that a properly chosen end will give a moral quality to the ways that we go about achieving it. For instance, suppose I choose the moral end of becoming an honest person. Any right-thinking person, I believe, will recognize this as a worthy goal. Obviously the only means whereby I can achieve this end of being an honest person is by performing honest deeds. By no stretch of the imagination can it be conceived that this end would justify dishonest behavior. Thus it is not that "the end justifies the means" is an open door to any sort of behavior; rather, the nature of the end communicates a specific character to the means and "justifies" them as functionally good in actualizing the chosen goal. Hence, the choice of the end is the decisive issue.

The second type of ethical theory emphasizes obedience and duty and says that one's ethical life is determined by law or commandment. This approach is called an "ethic of obligation." In its purest form this approach has no concern for the consequences of our ethical decisions, but only whether our motive for keeping the law is respect for the law.

Even though there is a superficial similarity between this type of ethics and casuistry, it is different because the law or imperative that dictates duty is nonspecific if properly derived and developed. It is sufficiently general or universal to be applicable to all ethical issues. The classic expression of this form of ethics is found in the famous "categorical imperative" of eighteenth-century philosopher Immanuel Kant.

In technical ethical terminology, the first approach is called *teleological* (from the Greek word *telos,* meaning purposive end), and the second is called *deontological* (a term applied to it by nineteenth-century ethical philosopher Jeremy Bentham, using the Greek word *deon* for "ought" or "binding").

The question we must now address in relation to this distinction is whether Christian ethics is teleological or deontological in form. Is it an ethic of aspiration or of obligation? Christian ethical teachers are not fully agreed on this issue. Perhaps one reason is that the two views are not mutually exclusive. That is, it is possible that certain elements of both approaches are identified in Christian ethics.

Since guidelines for Christian behavior are grounded in the will of God, and people of his kingdom are called on to obey these guidelines, we clearly have a deontological dimension. But on the other hand, it seems clear that divinely revealed ethical guidelines are informed by a purpose or goal that God desires to accomplish in the lives of his people. So there is also a teleological element.

After many years of reflection on the classical philosophical models of these ethical types (Aristotle = teleological and Kant = deontological) I have come to the conclusion that Christian ethics, especially when viewed from a Wesleyan perspective, is thoroughgoingly teleological. A careful study of John Wesley's own ethical instruction reveals that he self-consciously understood ethics in this fashion.[7] In fact his whole understanding of the Christian life is cast in these terms, and he repeatedly points out that the end *(telos)* that God is seeking to produce in our lives is a renewal of the divine image. Thus Wesley defines the essence of the Christian life as the divine activity of renewing human persons in the image of God. Here, I believe, is the clue to a proper understanding of Christian ethics.

A further analysis of Wesley's view of sanctification will reinforce this conclusion. One of his central categories, which he developed reluctantly because of its potential distortion, was Christian perfection. The idea of Christian perfection has historically been taught as an ideal, an ever receding goal.[8] It is doubtless because of this historical pattern that Albert Outler makes the comment that "it is generally agreed, in the history of ethics and moral theory, that deontology and Christian perfection do not mix readily."[9]

Outler admits that in the light of Wesley's obsession with "ideas about Christian discipline and duty . . . his wide assortment of 'rules,' together with his incessant exhortations to Christian morality, . . . it does seem obvious that Wesley must have been a deontologist in ethics—forever asking about the *ought* in moral issues, about one's *duty* or about the rules for authentic Christian living." However, he insists that this is not the case.[10] Actually, Wesley's rules functioned in a teleological context as prudential means to move the believer toward the goal of an ever more perfect conformity to the image of God as embodied in Jesus Christ.

Many of Wesley's successors in the American Holiness movement unfortunately turned this teleological emphasis into a deontological one.[11] But the reason for this in large part was the polemical situation in the nineteenth century. Among mainline Methodists in particular there was a correlative decline of traditional moral standards and the emphasis on "entire sanctification" as a present experience. In the light of this, advocates of "the second blessing" tended to preach and teach it as a "perfected perfection," that is, that the moment of entire sanctification is a destination rather than a step on the Christian pilgrimage toward the final perfection.[12] This emphasis was stultifying to further spiritual growth and tended to lose the dynamic character of the Christian life that was indigenous to Wesley's own teaching and that gave to it a teleological flavor.[13] The corollary to the concept of a "perfected perfection" was an ethic that was deontological in nature.[14]

Wesley himself studiously avoided the sterility of this way of seeing Christian perfection by emphasizing a "perfectible perfection."[15] He strongly rejected the idea of what he called a "perfection of degrees," that is, "one that does not admit of continual increase."[16]

A further aspect of Wesley's teaching that supports this claim is his repeated emphasis on the correlation of holiness and happiness. This gives rise to Outler's confession that after years of studying Wesley, he was surprised to discover that "this man was a *eudaimonist,* convinced and consistent all his life. All his emphases on duty and discipline are auxiliary to his main concern for human *happiness,* (blessedness, etc.)."[17]

The issue hangs on how Wesley understood happiness. No argument is necessary to demonstrate that he was not a hedonist, or a naturalist like Aristotle, even though the proper meaning of *eudaimonism,* according to Aristotle, is "well-being," which lies close to what Wesley would have meant by the concept. Neither is he a utilitarian, identifying happiness with pleasure. Many of Wesley's definitions of important theological concepts are simply repetitions of biblical phrases. This is both safe and difficult since the student is left to exegete the meaning of those texts and then determine if this is consistent with the general movement of Wesley's thought.

This is true of Wesley's concept of happiness. In his sermon "The Way to the Kingdom" he says, "True religion, or a heart right toward God and man [note the dual dimension] implies happiness as well as holiness. For it is not only 'righteousness,' but also 'peace, and joy in the Holy Ghost.' " He goes on to state that "this holiness and happiness, joined in one, are sometimes styled, in the inspired writings, 'the Kingdom of God.' "[18]

But in a nearly philosophical statement he provides what could actually be formulated into a good connotative definition. Naturally, it is cast in theological terms. In seeking to answer the question about the "original state of the brute creation," he describes the first human's created state as being one in which he knew, loved and obeyed the Creator. His conclusion: "From this right state and right use of all his faculties, his happiness naturally flowed. In this the essence of his happiness consisted."[19]

Wesley's comments on happiness have a close affinity with Augustine's, who likewise spoke about beatitude as the ultimate quest of human persons, and for much the same reason as Wesley, a reason embodied in Wesley's doctrine of prevenient grace. Also like Augustine, Wesley believed that all persons seek happiness, but most do so in the wrong place. In speaking about Eve's tasting the forbidden fruit, he says her sin was seeking "a better way to happiness than God had taught her."[20]

If we are to grasp the significance of this correlation, we must understand Wesley's view of human nature, the subject of the next chapter.

PART II

THE IMAGE OF GOD AS ETHICAL BENCHMARK

Four

IMAGE OF GOD: DESTINY AND DISASTER

The biblical story opens with a theological statement about the origin of all things. It affirms that God is the source of all that is. Both creation sagas (Gen 1:1—2:4 and 2:4-25) are structured to convey that the apex of God's creative activity was human persons, which is confirmed by the affirmation that humankind is made in the image of God.

Although this explicit language is seldom used after these initial accounts, the truth of humankind's destiny is implicitly assumed throughout the Bible, which builds on the careful foundation laid by these early narratives. One of the important aspects of the nature of the *imago Dei* (image of God) is reflected in the precision of the biblical references. They do not say that humans *are* the image of God, but that they were made *in* the image of God. This suggests that while the image was perfect, it still needed to be actualized by living it out and developing its implication through experience. Each good decision the first human couple made enriched that image through experience.

This truth can be illustrated through the analogy of marriage. When two people stand before a minister to pledge their vows to each other, their love is perfect (or should be) in the sense that they have now excluded all other loves from their lives. But with the continuing experience of living together and developing their relationship, making adjustments and adaptations to each other, their "perfect" love grows and develops and is enriched through the years.

This analogy implies that the image is dynamic in character and is not to be interpreted in terms of some substantial entity or quality. As we will see shortly, the only conception that allows for this dynamic character is a relational model.

When we come to the New Testament we find a similar distinction that has far-reaching ethical implications. The language used of Jesus describes him as *the* image of God. He was the reality of God manifesting himself in human form (Rom 8:29; 2 Cor 4:4; Col 1:15). This language stands in contrast to the way humanity is described as being made *in* the image of God. The relation between these two forms of expression is well stated by Philip Edgecombe Hughes: "The Son himself is the image in or according to which man was created; that is to say, the Son *is* the Image of God. . . . He is not *in* the image of God, for it is man the creature who is formed in that image."[1]

This distinction has a dual implication. One clear implication is that Christ as the image of God is the ethical ideal. For the authentic Christian believer the dominant ethical drive is to be conformed to the character of Christ. Christ embodies God's creative destiny for humankind. Such an incarnation was essential because of the Fall and the consequent need for a reedition of God's original intention for humankind to replace the Fall's distortion. Christ is the image in which humankind was initially created and embodies the destiny to which we are called.

The second implication is that from a biblical perspective the ideal of the image of God is an "impossible possibility" for humankind. That is, we can never become fully and completely what Christ *is*. While a truly Christian attitude presses toward the mark, it must always be accompanied by the disclaimer "not that I have already obtained all this, or have already been made perfect" (Phil 3:12).

Wesley, Sanctification and the *Imago Dei*

For John Wesley the essence of sanctification is the renewal of humankind in the image of God. Few concepts, if any, appear more frequently in his published sermons. Every aspect of the redemptive activity of God in human life is at some time referred to in this way, including *regeneration, entire sanctification* and *growth in grace*. He, as well as all authentic Wesleyan theology, recognizes the lifelong quest for fuller conformity to the image that is an essential component of the biblical doctrine of sanctification. Perhaps this is why many Wesleyan hymns dealing with sanctification are hymns of aspiration.

This is not to deny the reality of a decisive encounter with God in which one can be perfected in love, a concept Wesleyan theology is also committed to. But there is a significant distinction between ethical perfection and perfection in love, a distinction made in Scripture in phrases such as "without fault" (Jude 24) and "blameless" (Eph 1:4) and affirmed in various ways throughout the history of Christian spirituality.[2] Wesley simply recovered and gave a distinctive expression to a long-standing tradition in Christian teaching.

Alongside this teaching, and sometimes overshadowing it, is the Wesleyan belief that broadly understood, sanctification is a lifelong process that moves along by stages. Or, as Bishop Moule put it when referring to "entire sanctification," "It is a crisis with a view to a process."[3] One can so define *sanctification* as to eliminate the progressive element and restrict its meaning exclusively to the moment known in Wesleyan circles as entire sanctification, but this is to fly in the face of both Scripture and classical Christian theology, and it cannot be taken seriously.

To properly understand the significance of the *imago Dei* as humankind's created destiny, we must give close attention to its meaning.

The Image as Relationship

Through the centuries theologians have offered several different interpretations of the meaning of *imago Dei*. Unfortunately much of this theorizing was done more in light of Greek philosophy than in light of biblical texts, which resulted in merely attempting to show how humans differed from the lower orders of nature. The classical answer to this distinctive feature focused on humans' rational nature, reason. Aristotle's definition became the touchstone of theological interpretation: "Man is a rational animal." In theological thought this is considered a definition from below. This is not to deny that the image of God differentiates humankind from all else in the created world, but it is an error to *define* the image from this perspective.

Ethicist Paul Ramsey critiques this approach by pointing out its tendency to blur the distinction between humankind and God. Seeking to provide a barrier against a naturalistic reduction of humanity to the level of physical or animal nature, definitions from below fall into the error of exalting the human to the level of the divine. They assert discontinuity between humankind and nature in such a fashion as to overlook or understate the discontinuity between the human and God.[4]

It is a startling truth that modern theological scholars have only recently begun listening to the biblical texts, and Karl Barth can take a large part of the credit for this. But once this "Copernican revolution" occurred, virtually all contemporary biblical and theological scholars recognized the inadequacy of exploring the question "from below" and have begun to seek the solution "from above." This approach has resulted in a widespread consensus that the proper way to understand the image of God is in terms of relationship.[5] Paul Ramsey argues that "in the course of Christian thought, most of the decisive and distinctive Christian interpretations of man have been of this sort" and includes Paul, Augustine, Kierkegaard and Barth as examples.

It may take some effort to begin thinking in this way, since common sense seems to point in a different direction. As J. N. D. Kelly noted in discussing Augustine's relational interpretation of the Trinity,

> To modern people, unless schooled in technical philosophy, the notion of relations (e.g., "above," "to the right of," "greater than") as having

a real subsistence sounds strange, although they are usually prepared to concede their objectivity, i.e., that they exist in their own right independent of the observer. . . . The advantage of the theory from [Augustine's] point of view was that, by enabling him to talk meaningfully about God at a new language level, it made it possible simultaneously to affirm unity and plurality of the Deity without lapsing into paradox.[6]

It is easier to think of the image as *something* in humanity's makeup, such as reason or personality, than as a relation. But I hope that as the implications of this way of thinking unfold, it will become increasingly clear how adequate, practical and biblical it is, and consequently, how much easier to think about.

Several contemporary thinkers have seriously engaged the biblical text and concluded that the image of God involves a fourfold relationship: with God, with others, with the earth and with self. Most scholars include only the first three, but a few, including myself, see the fourth relationship as an essential component of the first three. That is, the role of the self is the determining factor in whether or not the threefold relation is in place or out of place.

The primary relation constituting the *imago Dei* is humanity's relation to God, in the sense that a person's right relation to others and the earth is dependent on a right relation to God (see chapter seven). But there is an interrelation among these aspects such that any one of them impinges on each of the others.

Understood as the basis for ethics, this structure encompasses all possible ethical questions from a religious perspective. Although he states it in significantly different terms, H. Orton Wiley, perhaps the most influential theologian in the Holiness movement, recognizes much the same structure in the section on ethics in his *Christian Theology*. Wiley's view of Christian ethics is quite different from the one developed here, but the important point is his recognition of the relationships that define the ethical life.[7]

Christopher J. H. Wright, in an exceptionally insightful study of Old Testament ethics, offers the following analysis. His premise is that the theology and ethics of the Old Testament are inseparable and that a knowledge of theology will provide us with the framework of Old Testament ethics. This means that by this method we can identify the principle that informs the multitude of laws and ethical guidance found throughout the Old Testament.

> Old Testament ethics are built upon Israel's understanding of who and what they were as a people, of their relationship to God and of their physical environment—their land. These were the three primary factors of their theology and ethics. God, Israel and the land, in a triangle of relationships, each of which affected the other.[8]

Using the imagery of a triangle, he identifies the three basic principles of Old Testament ethics as the theological angle, the social angle and the economic angle, which corresponds to the relationships that constitute what it means for human beings to be made in the image of God.

The *Imago* in Genesis 1—2

A further insight into the ethical implications of the image of God are seen by exploring, on the basis of the "state of integrity" depicted in Genesis 1—2, the nature of this web of relations we have introduced. Dietrich Bonhoeffer referred to the threefold aspect of the *imago* in terms of freedom, a term needing explanation since it is easily misunderstood. Bonhoeffer explains it as follows:

> Freedom is not something man has for himself but something he has for others. No man is free "as such," that is, in a vacuum, in the way that he may be musical, intelligent or blind as such. Freedom is not a quality of man, nor is it an ability, a capacity, a kind of being that somehow flares up in him. Anyone investigating man to discover freedom finds nothing of it. Why? because freedom is not a quality which can be revealed—it is not a possession, a presence, an object, nor is it a form for existence—but a relationship and nothing else. In

truth, freedom is a relationship between two persons. Being free means "being free for the other," because the other has bound me to him. Only in relationship with the other am I free.[9]

Bonhoeffer uses certain prepositions that can be inserted nicely into the relationship web: "freedom *for* God," "freedom *for* the other" and "freedom *from* the earth." Including the relation to self in this scheme would give us "freedom *from* self," meaning freedom from self-domination.

The concept of openness may make even clearer the divinely intended relation to God and others. Since these relationships entail reciprocity, it might seem as if this term would not directly apply to the earthly dimension. However, several theologians have argued that such a relation may and should exist. Following the implications of Martin Buber's "I-Thou" exposition of interpersonal relations, Douglas John Hall argues for communion with nonhuman nature and deplores the objectification of nature that makes this possibility questionable. He says, "So successful was Christian education in objectifying the natural order that students of theology, charmed though they may be by Martin Buber's *I and Thou* as a way of discussing divine-human and human-human relationships, are invariably amused to find Buber insisting that it is possible to have an I-Thou relationship with a tree and a cat."[10]

The word *love* is not found in the Genesis account, but it is a theme that is developed throughout the "whole tenor of Scripture" and can serve as a description of this relation: love for God, love for the other person and love for the earth.

One of the most significant theological terms in the Old Testament is *shalom*. While commonly thought of as meaning simply "peace," it much more adequately carries the connotation of holistic well-being, a comprehensive concept that includes all the relationships we have identified. Elmer Martens defines *shalom* as it is depicted in the Garden of Eden: "The state of *shalom* is one of inward and outward peace, material and spiritual satiation, harmony of an individual with himself, with nature, with the world of people, and clearly with God, the Creator."[11]

The *Imago* and Original Sin

The idyllic pictures in Genesis 1—2 turn sour when we get to chapter 3. Eve is approached by a sinister figure symbolized by a serpent, the standard symbol of evil in much early literature, such as the Babylonian account of the Fall. Faced with the delightful prospect of eating the forbidden fruit and becoming like God, she yielded to temptation and enticed Adam to do the same. In Hebrew theology the etiological character of the story is obvious. Its purpose is to explain the origin of the human predicament. Whether one views it as a "once upon a time" event or the "story of everyman," the end result is the same, a disruption of the relationships that constitute the *imago Dei.* That disruption is the essence of the human predicament. It is, in traditional language, the essence of sin.

The self plays a major role in this disaster. Whereas Adam and Eve at first recognized and accepted their creaturely status, now they have intended to usurp the place of God, and self is elevated to the position of sovereignty. Fear of the divine presence intruded into their consciousness. No longer could they feel comfortable with the thought of an intimate relationship with the LORD God, so when they heard the "sound of the LORD God walking in the garden in the cool of the day . . . they hid from the LORD God among the trees of the garden" (Gen 3:8).

The "freedom for God" had now been replaced by fear and anxiety, the openness had turned into secretiveness. Now they were unable to look God in the eye because they had renounced his lordship in their lives, and this was the only basis on which there could be communion between Creator and creature.

The consequence of this "revolt against heaven" was expulsion from the Garden, which had been the symbol of communion, and provisions were made to bar their reentry into this relation on their own initiative.

Likewise, as they existentially experienced alienation from God, the relation of openness between the couple was also disrupted. The absence of clothes in the state of integrity bespeaks a radical openness, free from the lust that seeks self-gratification without regard for the personhood of the other. So their putting on of protective garments was a symbol of a brokenness that can never be fully restored for us in this existence. The core of relationship disruption revolves around a false position of the self in relation to the other person. Lust, jealousy, anger, suspicion and other manifestations of sin intrude into the picture as a result of narcissism. This alienation of people from each other is highlighted early on in the human story in the fratricide involving Cain and Abel. The heinousness is enhanced by the fact that they were brothers who became enemies (at least from Cain's side) over religion. The Babel incident also underscores the alienation from others that is a central feature of the human predicament. The absence of communication resulted in a physical dispersion that pointed only to a deeper alienation.

Arthur Holmes points to this truth in his description of human personhood vis-à-vis the most intimate of relations, the husband-wife union.

If I relate to my wife as to an object, I to it, then I dominate her and use and repress her, and remain closed to what she could be to herself. But if we relate to each other as persons, subject to subject with trust and openness and mutuality, then communication develops, as does friendship. This is egalitarian, equal persons equally respected and equally responsible. It evokes love, not the *eros* that desires for oneself, often selfishly, but the *agape* that gives of oneself in serving the other. Such relationships to other persons are the matrix where freedom and responsibility come alive. I become my brother's keeper, and he becomes mine.[12]

In the same fashion, Adam's relation to the earth is now one of alienation. His primary responsibility for caretaking is not removed, but now the task becomes much more difficult because Adam's declaration of independence from God has resulted in the earth's declaration of independence from humankind's dominion. Although this curse is cast in agricultural terms in Genesis 3:17-19, it extends to all the products of the earth as developed by humankind. In a most graphic description of the consequences of this aspect of the Fall, Dietrich Bonhoeffer pictures the inability of humans to maintain control of the earth due to their own perversity.

We . . . try to rule, but it is the same here as on Walpurgis Night.[13] We think we are pushing and we are being pushed. We do not rule, we are ruled. The thing, the world, rules man. Man is a prisoner, a slave of the world, and his rule is illusion. Technology is the power with which the earth grips man and subdues him. And because we rule no more, we lose ground, and then the earth is no longer *our* earth, and then we become strangers on earth. We do not rule because we do not know the world as God's creation, and because we do not receive our dominion as God-given but grasp it for ourselves.[14]

As Bonhoeffer suggests, the elevation of self to the false position of sovereign has once again been identified as the source of the problem. This analysis reinforces the understanding of sin dominant in classical Christian thought. It is basically egocentricity or self-centeredness. Augustine referred to it as pride or hubris. Martin Luther spoke of sin as man "curved in upon himself." It is this self-centeredness, manifested in variegated forms, that stands as the barrier to a return to humankind's created destiny. It resists submission to God, since it is not subject to the law of God. It destroys personal relations because of anger, jealousy, exploitation or a plethora of other forms of self-assertion, and it appropriates the resources of the earth for its own selfish ends.

Imago—Totally Lost or Merely Marred?

Before we can grasp the broader picture of the ethical perspectives that inform Scripture, we must explore further the implications of the Fall. This involves the question of the loss of the image of God. Was it totally destroyed, or was there some reflection of it remaining, even in fallen humanity? If we look closely, the Bible itself will provide us the answer to this question.

In Genesis 9:6, shortly after the great flood, we find that murder is prohibited on the basis that God has created humankind in his own image. This leaves us with the clear indication that the Fall has not totally effaced the *imago Dei*. But when we turn to the New Testament we find several passages (see Rom 8:29; 2 Cor 3:18) that suggest that God's redemptive intention is to restore humanity to the lost image. Are we looking at a contradiction, or is there something theologically significant in this polarity?

Actually, the only way one can make sense out of the "whole tenor of Scripture" is by recognizing that in one sense the image was retained after the Fall and in another sense it was lost at the Fall. Christian theology has recognized this from at least the second century A.D. While it has been expressed in different ways, some more adequate that others, there have been only a very few leading Christian thinkers who have not taught that the image was both lost and retained at one and the same time, and they were unable to sustain this position.

For many years Irenaeus's distinction between the image and likeness, based on a faulty exegesis of Genesis 1:26, was the standard way of identifying the twofold aspect of the image of God. It became one major aspect of the so-called medieval synthesis developed by Thomas Aquinas in his monumental *Summa*.[15]

Another very popular method was to distinguish between the natural and the moral image. The moral image was lost in the Fall but the natural image, though marred, was retained. As some contemporary theology has correctly recognized, this distinction has several problems with it, including the word *natural*. If the image is natural, it is not "of God" in the distinctive sense intended, and thus the term *natural image* is a contradiction in terms.

In the Wesleyan perspective the *imago* was totally lost as a consequence of the Fall, but a reflection of it (in the pattern described earlier) is restored by the activity of prevenient grace. In fact it is this graciously restored aspect of the *imago* that constitutes personhood. This presupposes what contemporary studies of human beings have affirmed, namely that personhood is a relational category. In the words of John Macmurray in his Gifford Lectures, we are "Persons in Relations."[16]

Christian sociologist Tony Campolo describes in his book *A Reasonable Faith* a conversation he had with one of his graduate students:

Without human interaction you would have no language with which to think. You would have no categories with which to interpret reality. All the traits that you listed in your attempt to describe humanness to me would be lacking. You would not even have a consciousness of self, for without social relationships you would never develop the reflective capacities that are essential for self-awareness. It is only by adopting the perspective of a significant other that you become conscious that you are an existing person. In short, without interaction with human beings you would have the form of a man, but none of the traits. Your humanity is a gift of society. You become what the people who socialize you are.[17]

Beyond the sociological explanation is the theological idea that personhood is an ontological category that is possible only in relation, and that involves the web of relations that we have identified as constituting the *imago Dei*. It is the activity of prevenient grace that restores a "vestige" of those relations and that provides a barrier to prevent humanity from lapsing completely into the subhuman.

Western theology has followed the definition of *person* proposed by Boethius in the sixth century. He defined *person* as "an individual subsistence of a rational nature." The result of this definition is a dualism between nature and grace, so that it becomes difficult to define *person* theologically, that is, in relation to God. It also contributed to a strong sense of individualism, since "substance" is a self-contained entity incapable of relation. It furthermore opened the door to a purely secular or naturalistic view of personhood that became a reality under the influence of the Enlightenment.[18]

This somewhat odd truth that the *imago* is both lost and retained (or restored) at one and the same time suggests that the ethical question has two dimensions. If the image retained is that which makes humanity unique, different from animals or other forms of created life, it points to the possibility that there is an ethic that pertains to humankind as such, an ethic that is a reflection of the very structure of personhood. Since this structure is built into humankind by the creative activity of God, we may refer to the ethical dimensions of it as a *creation ethic.*

But the major thrust of Scripture and the Christian faith is that God wants to "reverse" the consequences of the Fall and restore humankind to the "lost estate," to full personhood, a fullness that is present in history only in Jesus of Nazareth. This involves two activities of divine grace: liberating humanity from the bondage of sin and renewing it in the divine image. We describe the first action by terms such as *reconciliation, justification, deliverance* or, perhaps most appropriately, *redemption,* which literally means "to buy back." The second movement of grace, the ethical aspect, we refer to as *sanctification.* Since sanctification centrally refers to the living out of the redeemed life, we may refer to the sanctified life as entailing a *redemption ethic.*

In light of this analysis, a full understanding of Christian ethics has two aspects, and an adequate discussion of Christian ethics must take note of both. Since the central thrust of biblical ethics relates to the ethical life of a redeemed people, this will occupy most of our attention, and to it we turn next. However, as most Christian people today recognize, Christians have a social responsibility beyond the boundaries of the church. There is considerable diversity of opinion as to how this responsibility is to be implemented. This book's thesis is that the social responsibility of the people of God is based on the creation ethic. Consequently it becomes very important to understand both its nature and its content to avoid the confusion that is so widespread as we face the question of how we are to relate redemptively to a non-Christian world.

Five

SALVATION AS RESTORATION

As the book of Hosea dramatically emphasizes, God is God and not man (11:9), and therefore he did not abandon the "project" when Adam and Eve took the disastrous step that resulted in their alienation. Rather, as the early Genesis story recounts, the Creator immediately revealed his intention to address the problem by returning to the Garden as before, "as if" nothing had happened. This is one of the most beautiful pictures of God in the Bible. He is a God of grace, who does not wait for the first couple to discover their predicament but comes to them on his own initiative for the express purpose of making them aware of their self-imposed alienation from the Source of life. His question, "Where are you?" was not a searching for someone he could not find. In the words of Franz Delitzsch, "God seeks him, not because he is lost from his knowledge, but from his communion."[1] The question was intended to arouse in Adam a realization that he was now lost, and no remedy for this predicament could occur without this realization taking place. Hence the grace of God is celebrated on the very threshold of fallen human history.

From this we may confidently say that God's purpose from the beginning was a recovery of that which was lost, a restoration of humankind to the image of God. This way of viewing salvation is beautifully captured in a paragraph from John Wesley's sermon "The Righteousness of Faith": "It is wisdom to aim at the best end by the best means. Now the best end which any creature can pursue is, happiness in God. And the best end a fallen creature can pursue is, the recovery of the favor and image of God."[2]

The phrase "the favor and image of God" is found in several of Wesley's sermons. By it he is suggesting a twofold aspect of salvation, both having the nature of restoration. The first has to do with justification or reconciliation, and the second has to do with sanctification or, as he defines "real religion" in his sermon "The General Spread of the Gospel":

a restoration of man by Him that bruises the serpent's head, to all that the old serpent deprived him of; a restoration, not only to the favour but likewise to the image of God, implying not barely deliverance from sin, but the being filled with the fulness of God.[3]

This phrase furthermore indicates the Wesleyan view of the *ordo salutis* (order of salvation). It will be helpful in understanding the theological context for Christian ethics from the Wesleyan perspective to give a summary of this process of renewal. A good place to begin is the status of fallen humanity vis-á-vis the Creator, that is, natural man.

Natural Man

There is an inherent tension in Wesley's own formulations about the status of fallen humanity since he spoke of the *imago Dei* in traditional terms. The only qualification he made was to add a third dimension to the standard distinction between the so-called natural and the moral image. He introduced the concept of the political image by which he referred to humans as governing beings, meaning their capacity to rule over lower creatures. This shows that Wesley was aware of a fuller concept of the *imago* than the traditional formulations.

The tension arises out of Wesley's belief that the *imago* was totally lost in the Fall, with the result that natural man was completely devoid of the image of God. And furthermore, the primary way he describes the mitigation of this is not in terms of some native endowment retained (such as the "natural" image) but of the activity of divine grace. It is in the light of this latter vision that our analysis can lay claim to be consistently Wesleyan.

In his own descriptions of natural man, Wesley is at one with the Reformed view of the corruption of human nature. But he is concerned to provide an alternative to the doctrine of unconditional election by holding that prevenient grace is not coercive or irresistible. It extends to all human persons, restoring to them the capacity to respond to, as well as resist, the calling of God. Thus while he declares that natural man is devoid of both the knowledge of God and the ability to turn to God on his own motivation, both of these are graciously provided through God's initiative. Wesley's own words make his position clear.

Natural free-will, in the present state of mankind, I do not understand: I only assert, that there is a measure of free-will supernaturally restored to every man, together with that supernatural light which "enlightens every man that cometh into the world."[4]

From this statement it is clear that those who have accused Wesley of Pelagianism are sadly mistaken. He expressly denies this charge, and with good reason. Furthermore, those who suggest that only a doctrine of unconditional election and irresistible grace can legitimately lay claim to a doctrine of salvation by grace alone likewise fail to grasp Wesley's fine stipulation.

In this context we are able to see the validity of Wesley's own claim that he is but "a hair's breadth from Calvinism." In light of his insistence on the total depravity of human nature, the "hair" that distinguishes Wesleyan soteriology from Reformed is prevenient grace. Wesley's grim descriptions of natural man are qualified by his assertion that such portraits refer to persons without grace, but that there is no person anywhere or who has ever lived who is devoid of grace. In a word, "natural man" is a logical abstraction.

For allowing that all the souls of men are dead in sin by *nature*, this excuses none, seeing there is no man that is in a state of mere nature; there is no man, unless he has quenched the Spirit, that is wholly void of the grace of God. No man living is entirely destitute of what is vulgarly called *natural conscience*. But this is not natural: It is more properly termed, *preventing grace*.[5] Harald Lindström correctly points out that the idea of prevenient grace is in Wesley logically bound up with the Arminian view of election.[6]

Awakening and Repentance

The first step in the order of salvation, in the Wesleyan scheme, is awakening, by which is meant the arousing of the person to the realization of his or her lostness and need for salvation. As the quotation above makes clear, the most universal level of awakening occurs in terms of conscience. Hence, as Wesley never tires of asserting, there is a universal knowledge of God that not only renders all without excuse but also provides the basis for salvation if properly responded to.

In its distinctively Christian function, awakening is the activity of the Spirit that arouses one's consciousness of need in relation to the work of Jesus Christ. The Spirit convinces the unbeliever of his or her sin in relation to the crucified Christ and thus the need for salvation, that he or she is lost, and that this is the direct result of rejecting Christ (Jn 16:8-11).

When the awakening work of the Spirit is properly responded to, it results in repentance, which for Wesley means self-knowledge. In fact, awakening and repentance are so closely related in meaning that the concepts can almost be used interchangeably.

This soteriological activity of prevenient grace distinguishes the Wesleyan *ordo salutis* from the Reformed view when its implications are consistently followed. While there has been a significant Armini-anizing of the traditional Reformed position so that relatively few "five-point" Calvinists still exist, when its fundamental presuppositions are logically spelled out, the Reformed order begins with regeneration, not awakening and repentance. Since the "call" is extended only to the elect, and since there is no gracious basis for that call being heard by any but the elect, and the elect are so "dead in sin" as to have no prior possibility of response, a spiritual "resurrection" must occur as the first movement of grace in the human soul. Thus regeneration precedes repentance and faith.[7]

Faith and Justification

Early in his spiritual pilgrimage Wesley followed the path that Albert Outler refers to as "the way of moral rectitude." His trek to America, his pursuit of discipline in the "Holy Club" and his efforts to live a moral life generally were pursued in view of acceptance with God. But in the Aldersgate experience on May 31, 1738, he came to see and experience for the first time the truth of justification by faith alone. As he began to preach this in his subsequent sermons he encountered opposition, and his journal records several instances where he spoke of preaching this message but was asked not to preach in that place again. Nonetheless, this understanding of how one comes into a saving relation with God became the authoritative teaching of the Wesleyan revival.

Justification is the metaphor that describes entering into a restored relation to God in a more or less external sense. Wesley refers to it as "a relative change" and insists that it should be distinguished from sanctification, which he consistently defines as "a real change." As we have noted earlier, he resists both the Catholic view and the traditional Protestant view of justification as being either the result of works-righteousness or the result of a "legal fiction." Thus justification is the gateway into the Christian life proper, which is centered in the general concept of sanctification. Lindström correctly points out that Wesley's central concept of salvation is a "restoration to health," based on his thoroughgoing view of original sin. He comments: "A conception of religion which accepts such a view of sin must be determined by the idea of sanctification. And this is the case with Wesley."[8]

Sanctification

Wesley describes the nature of sanctification as a "real change," and this change is always seen as ethical in nature. His generic definition of it is "being renewed in the image of God."

Based on these terms, the beginning of sanctification occurs in the new birth, continues in a lifelong process of transformation that is teleological in nature and is marked along the path by certain specific stages, the most notable of which Wesley refers to as entire sanctification. Wesley's favorite description of this process is embodied in a phrase borrowed from Paul in Galatians 5:6, "faith expressing itself through love."

It has been legitimately argued that the essence of Wesley's understanding of the content of sanctification is to be seen in terms of love.[9] The clearest distinction between the various phases of the lifelong process may be found in his sermon "On Patience":

> Love is the sum of Christian sanctification; it is the one *kind* of holiness, which is found, only in various *degrees,* in the believers who are distinguished in St. John into "little children, young men, and fathers." The difference between one and the other properly lies in the degree of love. And herein there is as great a difference in the spiritual, as in the natural sense, between fathers, young men, and babies.[10]

Here we see Wesley's emphasis on the continuity of the Christian life and that this continuity is to be interpreted in terms of love. This spiritual maturation is not merely the result of human discipline but, as with all Wesleyan understanding of the divine-human relation, is synergistic in nature. It involves the interaction between sovereign grace and human response. This distinctive character may be seen in a further statement from the same sermon.

> In the same proportion as he grows in faith, he grows in holiness; he increases in love, lowliness, meekness, in every part of the image of God; till it pleases God, after he is thoroughly convinced of inbred sin, of the total corruption of his nature, to take it all away; to purify his heart and cleanse him from all unrighteousness; to fulfill that promise

which he made first to his ancient people, and in them to the Israel of God in all ages: "I will circumcise thy heart, and the heart of thy seed, to love the Lord thy God with all thy heart, and with all thy soul."[11] Wesley persistently rejected the charge that he was teaching "sinless perfection." With sure insight he recognized the New Testament perspective concerning all religious experience. The New Testament teaching about the duality of the kingdom as both present and future results in the believer's being no longer what he or she was but not yet what he or she will be at the consummation. Hence the claim for the possibility of "perfect love" in entire sanctification never led to a stultification of the Christian life but merely brought to clearer focus the *telos* of the *imago Dei,* which was the ultimate goal of the total process and which intensifies one's commitment to the pursuit of that goal. Interestingly, Wesley himself thought this was a goal that would remain an alluring prospect even after the probation of this life was past. One can only hope that he was right.

Six

CHRISTIAN ETHICS: FOR THE PEOPLE OF GOD

T he first appearance in Scripture of the terms *salvation* and *saved* is in connection with Israel's deliverance at the Reed Sea (Ex 14:13, 30). They saw their enemies dead before their faces, the threat of slavery in the past and recognized that they were "saved." The term itself means "to be wide, spacious, to be free."[1] Its use in the context of the exodus reinforces the idea that salvation implies deliverance.

If we trace the idea of salvation throughout Scripture, we find that this implication remains constant. The theme becomes central to the ministry of Jesus, illustrated by his miracles, especially the casting out of demons. In the New Testament deliverance is no longer understood in terms of national liberty effected by the destruction of threatening foreign nations but in terms of liberation from "demonic powers," resulting in a spiritual freedom.[2]

One of the major New Testament images for the work of Christ is that of victor (see Col 2:15). Gustaf Aulén has sought to rehabilitate this theme in the modern world under the rubric "Christus Victor." As Aulén clearly demonstrates, it was a popular idiom in the early church. Although many moderns may find it difficult to accept the New Testament's depiction of this explanation, anyone who recognizes the power of addiction in its multifaceted forms should be able to see the highly relevant features of Christ's work as deliverer.[3]

Ethics as Response to Grace

The implication of the biblical concept of salvation is that God's saving intention for the human race involves first a deliverance from bondage. This deliverance is uniformly understood as an overture of grace. But after God has graciously acted to effect the deliverance of those in bondage, he then calls them to a specific lifestyle as a response to his grace. The exodus itself illustrates this. As Christopher J. H. Wright says in a discussion of Old Testament ethics,

> The sequence of events in the Biblical story is very important. God did not send Moses down to Egypt with the law already tucked under his cloak to say to Israel in bondage, "Here you are. This is God's law, and if you keep it fully from now on, God will rescue you out of this slavery."[4]

After Moses led the Hebrew slaves from the site of deliverance to Mount Sinai, the process of finalizing that act began. It involved offering to them the possibility of becoming the people of the Lord, of entering into a covenant with him. Like the act of deliverance itself, the covenant was offered as an act of grace that apparently could have been rejected. But acceptance of this relationship with the Redeemer called for a responsible lifestyle on their part, just as God was committing himself to them in certain ways on his part. Hence the law was not the basis for the covenant. It set forth the guidelines for their loving response to the grace of God within the covenant relation.

One of the unique features of the Ten Commandments is that unlike many or most codes of law, no sanctions are attached to them. One of them is reinforced by a promise, but no punishment or penalty is stated for disobeying them. The sanction precedes, rather than follows, their statement. The reason for keeping these is not the negative consequences that follow if they are broken, but the context in which they are given. The God who delivered his people from oppression gave these words, and the deliverance itself was sufficient reason for living this kind of life.

Here we have the pattern for biblical ethics. The law was given to Israel subsequent to their deliverance as a guide to the life they are to live "as delivered people." In a word, from the biblical perspective ethics is a response to grace. Oswald Chambers speaks of salvation by grace as a "grand marvelous fact," and adds, "But Jesus says we have got to say 'Thank you' for our salvation, and the 'Thank you' is that our righteousness is to exceed the righteousness of the most moral man on earth."[5]

The Old Testament has often been misunderstood on this point. Like the New Testament, the Old Testament emphasizes that restoration of the divine-human relation is God's initiative. It is not the result of human beings searching for and finding God on their own. It is not the result of a moral life that creates a status of worthiness to be God's people.

Salvation and the Ethical Life

When we turn to the New Testament, whether the Gospels or the epistles, we find the same pattern. Salvation is by grace, not works, but the people of God who are saved are called to respond by an ethical life. The oft-repeated word in Paul's ethical comments is *therefore*. It is woven throughout his letters, even at times providing the structure of those letters. We have been "saved"; therefore, he emphasizes, live out this saved existence. Paul's frequent use of the imperative in tandem with the indicative implies "become what you are."

Few truths have been more difficult to maintain in the thinking of the church. We tend to get the cart before the horse and speak of being saved in terms of a change of lifestyle. Perhaps this is natural since genuine salvation is accompanied by a transformation that is quite often easy to recognize. But theologically that lifestyle change is the result, not the cause, of the person's salvation.

Notice the way Paul addressed ethical issues. He found numerous occasions to critique the behavior of the people in the churches to which he wrote. But, with one exception, never did he "un-Christianize" anyone for ethical deviations. This one exception was a flagrant flaunting of common morality that was generally approved by the accepted mores of decent society (1 Cor 5:1-5). In all other cases Paul pointed out that they were not living a life consistent with their profession of faith in Jesus Christ and called them to "become what they were." Paul knew that we are neither saved nor lost on the basis of our ethics. He knew equally well that the genuinely saved person should manifest a Christian lifestyle. Balancing these two truths is very difficult to maintain in both our thinking and our living, but if we do not do so we will have a distorted understanding of Christian ethics.

Redemption Ethics
A further qualification needs to be made on the basis of this understanding of ethics as a response to grace. "Redemption ethics" is for the people of God. The Ten Commandments, the Sermon on the Mount and other ethical Scripture passages are intended to be implemented by believers. They are not addressed to nonbelievers. We misunderstand their purpose and nature if we attempt to impose them on persons who are outside the faith. As Robert Chiles's insightful principle states, "It seems clear that a particular formulation cannot be imposed successfully on a religious disposition to which it is essentially alien."[6]

This point is clearly made in the instructions a father is to give to his child when the youth inquires, "What is the meaning of the stipulations, decrees and laws the LORD our God has commanded you?" (Deut 6:20). Lawrence Toombs summarizes the appropriate response this way:

> The father is to reply with a narrative of the deliverance of Israel from slavery in Egypt. The Law has its significance, then, only in the context of a relationship established by Yahweh with his people through an unexpected and gracious act of deliverance. It is the witness to and the consequence of that relationship; it has no meaning for or binding

power on anyone who stands outside that relationship.[7]

This presupposition, an essential Wesleyan premise as well as a biblical one, distinguishes a Wesleyan ethic from the majority of contemporary treatments. Even though numerous insights may be garnered from such works, the failure to recognize this biblical emphasis leads such treatments to fatal flaws. Apart from a living faith the church is but a religious club; apart from a personal conversion the so-called Christian is not profoundly committed to the goal of Christian ethics, that is, with all his or her being. This is not to suggest that conversion must take place according to the pattern of frontier revivalism, but it must entail a radical reorientation of one's life.

This too is a major emphasis of the book of Deuteronomy, which is often misunderstood as a legalistic document. There is a twofold emphasis in the book that invalidates this criticism. The first is the affirmation that the law is not foreign to human nature but is the normal expression of it, a truth we have seen to be native to the Wesleyan perspective. Basing his idea on Deuteronomy 30:11-14, Toombs says,

> The proper home of the Law is not in heaven, like the Tablets of Destiny of Babylonian mythology, or across the sea, like the land of immortality in Sumerian and Egyptian literature. The Law resides on earth in the quiet and intimate recesses of the human heart, from which man's outward actions arise. Therefore, since the Law is native, as it were, to human nature itself, it lays no impossible obligations upon man; it *can* be obeyed.[8]

The second emphasis is that keeping the law is not the result of human striving but of divine activity. This truth is presented in terms of the sign of the covenant relation—circumcision. Although the external sign may be present, because of a rebellious heart the person may still stand outside the covenant, but the "true mark of the Covenant, its sign and symbol, is within and not upon the visible, physical body."[9] Deuteronomy 30:6 makes this clear: "The LORD your God will circumcise your hearts and the hearts of your descendants, so that you may love him with all your heart and with all your soul, and live." This is one of John Wesley's favorite passages to support his faith in the transforming power of grace in sanctification.

Wesley's expositions of the Beatitudes emphasizes the same point. He interprets the first three as "removing the hindrances of true religion," which is uniformly defined as righteousness, or "the image of God" being renewed. He affirms that "the root of religion lies in the heart, in the inmost soul; that this is the union of the soul with God, the life of God in the soul of man," and goes on to relate this to the ethical life by saying that "if the root be really in the heart it cannot but put forth branches."[10]

In discourse six he refers to this "inward religion" that constitutes that "holiness without which no man shall see the Lord" as flowing from a "living faith in God through Jesus Christ."[11] Once the hindrances such as pride, levity and thoughtlessness, anger, impatience, and discontent are removed, "the native appetite of a heaven-born spirit returns, it hungers and thirsts after righteousness," namely, the image of God or "the mind that was in Christ Jesus."[12]

Late-nineteenth-century liberalism attempted to reduce Christianity to the ethical teaching of Jesus.[13] Speaking out against the inadequacy of this revisionism, Oswald Chambers dramatically highlighted the necessity for a prior deliverance before we take on the ethical challenges of Jesus' teaching.

If He is a Teacher only, then He is a most cruel Teacher, for He puts ideals before us that blanch us white to the lips and lead us to a hell of despair. But if He came to do something else as well as teach—if he came to re-make us on the inside and put within us His own disposition of unsullied holiness, then we can understand why He taught like He did.[14]

One important stipulation must be made in light of the Wesleyan *via media* between justification and sanctification. Even believers cannot look on ethical directions as rules that must be kept perfectly in order to experience the favor of God. Such an outlook can lead only to anxiety and fearfulness or else to hypocrisy.

Far too many sensitive Christians live a life of fear because of the flaws in their behavior, and they constantly question their status before God. While it is true that we cannot flagrantly ignore God's will, as Paul insisted in Romans 6:1-7, we are always justified by faith, not just initially. We should gain great comfort from the knowledge that each moment of every day God accepts us just as we are, even with our shortcomings and failures. This truth of grace should be a liberating experience, while at the same time it should be accompanied by an ethical seriousness characterized by a commitment to faithfully pursuing God's will for our life.

The Nature of Law

The response to grace is given guidance by the law, and it is important to recognize that the law of the believer's life finds its source in God. It is not derived from the surrounding culture, from family mores or even from the church, but from God himself. This presupposes that there is a personal God who is the creator of human life and who has an ideal for humankind that he has built into the structure of human personhood. It further presupposes that God has or will reveal that ideal in such a way that we may apprehend and embody it.

During the late Middle Ages there was a debate between two schools of thought on this issue, which throws a lot of light on how we are to understand God as the source of ethical standards. These two groups were known as voluntarists and intellectualists. Their debate was the result of projecting human psychology onto the divine nature. The discussion raged in human psychology about which was primary in human motivation, intellect or will. In other words, can we do right when we know it, or is the will too weak and in need of inner enablement in order to choose the right? The voluntarists said the will was primary, and even though we may come into possession of the knowledge of right and wrong, we will be unable to freely choose it. The intellectualists argued that to know the right is to do the right, and our basic need is for revelation.

Obviously in those terms the debate is not applicable to God. But when

God is considered the source of right and wrong, the issue is different. Are certain actions right because God wills (or commands) them to be so, or does God approve (will) certain actions as right because they are right in themselves? In other words, is right and wrong an expression of God's will or his nature? If the former, right and wrong are arbitrary and could conceivably be changed from time to time as God chose, thus leading to a sense of insecurity. If the latter, there would be a standard above God that determines right and wrong with which he simply concurs. It is a difficult issue to settle using these terms.

However, John Wesley insightfully spoke to the heart of the issue by suggesting that such a psychological analysis of God is inappropriate. When God wills, he said, it is God himself who is doing it.[15] But this does suggest that right and wrong as God reveals it to humankind is a manifestation of his nature and not an arbitrary imposition of commands and limitations. That is to say, God's ideals for human life are purposive.

This leads us to the question of the relation of the law to human nature. Is the law an imposition on human nature, or is it in some sense a means to humanization? The point to emphasize here is that God's law is at the same time the law of our created nature.

Many theologians, including John Wesley, taught that in his creation of humans God built a certain structure into us so that the law was synonymous with the constitution of human beings.[16] This suggests that God's ideal for humankind, if followed and lived out, will be fulfilling and not frustrating, liberating and not limiting. It is designed by him not to warp our humanity but to enhance it and actually make us more fully human, not less so. Wesley refers to the original inscription of the law given to unfallen humans as designed "to make way for a continual increase of their happiness; seeing every instance of obedience to that law would both add to the perfection of their nature and entitle them to an higher reward."[17]

When the law of human nature as designed by God was written down in the positive law, such as the Ten Commandments, it had the same purpose. Thus the Hebrew, who understood the nature of the Torah, did not look on it with fear or reluctance but embraced it with joy, since it was the law of his own being.

The place to see this joy and love for the law as anything but a galling imposition is in the psalms, which have been referred to as a devotional response to the law. In Psalm 1 the righteous and wicked are contrasted: the "blessed" man "delights" in the law and "meditates" on it day and night, with the result that he is "like a tree planted by streams of water" that "yields its fruit in season." The ungodly, the one who spurns the law of God, is "like chaff," and his life is empty of meaning. This same theme recurs in other psalms as well, especially Psalm 119.

Tony Campolo is right on target in relation to our contemporary secular culture when he says,

I think the gospel is about becoming human. . . . I think that being saved is realizing our potentiality for humanness rather than becoming otherworldly persons who find being *Homo sapiens* a real drag. . . . The theology that I developed in the context of discussion with my secular friends can properly be called "Christian humanism" and affirms that the achieving of the fullness of humanity is the ultimate end of all things and ultimately the will of God.[18]

Election, Mission and Ethics

To both the individual believer and to the church, the crucial importance of living an ethical life is seen by examining the biblical perspective on the reason God chose a special people. The people of God, whether Israel under the old covenant or the church under the new, have a clearly identifiable purpose for their existence. This purpose is embodied in the biblical concept of election.

The popular teaching of the doctrine of election among many evangelicals relates it to eternal destiny. That is, it is interpreted to mean that some persons are antecedently chosen to be ultimately saved and some to be finally lost. The oddity is that the teaching of this doctrine is often accompanied by a keen interest in and practice of evangelism, even though the two are logically exclusive.

But this view of election is derived by logical deduction from certain premises about the nature of God, premises that are antithetical to Wesleyan theology as well as to Scripture. It is not how the language of election is used in Scripture. In fact, nowhere in the Bible is election explicitly related to eternal destiny. Rather it is a concept that basically refers to God's choice of a person or a people to perform a task. That is to say, it is mission oriented. Old Testament theologian Theodorus C. Vriezen puts it succinctly: "Election means first of all that some one who is to perform a task is called upon and designated; to be elected implies special responsibility; it does not merely mean to be loved."[19]

This truth is explicitly stated in the opening of the redemptive story in Genesis 12:1-3, where God chooses Abraham and extends to him promises that include his being the source of a worldwide blessing. This is the clue as to why God chose Abraham and subsequently his descendants through Isaac and Jacob. They were to be the Lord's missionary people. This is woven like a golden thread throughout the Old Testament, reaching its culmination in the mission of the suffering servant (Isaiah 40—55) and lived out by Jesus.

An essential aspect of carrying out this mission, which was to be a witness to the true and living God, was the living of a lifestyle that would demonstrate to the world the redemptive intention of God. *Israel was to be God's paradigm of a redeemed people.* This is embodied in the preface to the Sinai covenant: "Now if you obey me fully and keep my covenant, then out of all nations you will be my treasured possession. Although the whole earth is mine, you will be for me a kingdom of priests and a holy nation" (Ex 19:5-6).

Christopher J. H. Wright makes a pertinent comment on this text: "Now if Israel as a nation were to be a priesthood, the implication is that they would represent God to the peoples of mankind in an analogous way. God's way would be made manifest in their life as a nation."[20] Thus the ethical standards proclaimed to God's people were his way of giving guidance to his purposes that were embodied in his original plan for the human race. And when Israel failed to live up to these ethical standards, as they so often did, it dishonored God and was a central failure on their part to carry out the mission for which they had been chosen.

As the new Israel, the church of Jesus Christ is called to the same mission. Now, however, the mission is seen in light of the life and ministry of Jesus Christ, who perfectly carried out the mission originally given to Israel but embodied now in one person. Thus the people called into being by the Holy Spirit on the basis of the Christ-event are elected to perpetuate that mission, to continue the work of Christ in the world. Luke's dedication that introduces the book of Acts implies that the work Jesus began is now to be continued through his Spirit-filled followers: "In my former book, Theophilus, I wrote about all that Jesus *began* to do and to teach" (1:1, emphasis added).

In this light it is easy to see how the mission of the church entails a lifestyle that is consistent with the profession of the name of Christ. The church cannot really be the church without ethical seriousness. By the same token, the one who professes the name of Christ is not an *authentic* believer without an accompanying ethical earnestness. This is the point of the book of James.

If one is to effectively implement this ethical commitment, he or she needs guidance. This brings us to the nitty-gritty of our subject. Where are we to find the insight to properly live the Christian life? What is really needed is a principle or set of principles ultimately derived from Scripture that will transcend the provincialisms of a rule book. The answer has been hinted at more than once, and now we must identify and elaborate it. The image of God is the reservoir of truth from which we can draw the ethical wisdom to be good disciples.

PART III

REDEMPTION ETHICS

Seven

THE IMAGE AS RELATION TO GOD

Several premises come together here to provide us with the distinctive understanding of Wesleyan ethics in regard to this aspect of the *imago Dei*. Sanctification, defined as the renewal of human persons in the image of God, is the bearer of ethics. The content of sanctification is quite uniformly described by Wesley in terms of love. While love is present in the believer's experience from the moment of the new birth, it is present in a "mixed" form (with self-love, love of the world, etc.),[1] but the movement of grace ideally brings one to the moment of "entire sanctification," which Wesley almost without exception defined as "the loving God with all the heart, soul, mind and strength and one's neighbor as oneself."

Love as an Ethical Category

In his sermon "The Way to the Kingdom" Wesley describes the kingdom as including "righteousness, and peace, and joy in the Holy Ghost." Righteousness—in this case ethical righteousness—is described in terms of the words of Jesus identifying "the two grand branches" of it, namely, the two love commandments. Love for God is the "first and great branch of Christian righteousness." Love for neighbor is the "second great branch of Christian righteousness," and is closely related to the first.[2]

This window into Wesley's thought world regarding the Christian life makes it clear that his is an ethic of love, and hence the love of (or for) God is the basic element in Christian ethics.

E. G. Sugden, editor of Wesley's *Standard Sermons,* has criticized Wesley at this point for, as he put it, failing to see that "love is the root, righteousness is the fruit." He justified Wesley's emphasis on the basis of the situation in eighteenth-century England where there was much emphasis on ethics but "little or nothing is said about the religious motive, the love to God and man, which alone makes morality in the fullest sense possible."[3]

Whether this criticism is justified remains to be seen. It is true that Wesley's exposition of the first commandment is normally rhetorical and devotional and the content is largely a collage of scriptural quotations, but does this mean that there is no normative ethical content involved? Actually, the summation of the first tablet of the law as set forth in the Shema (Deut 6:4-5) speaks in terms of undivided love for God, and Jesus is simply reiterating this Old Testament message. If we keep in mind that this ethic is for the people of God, perhaps there is more ethical content implied than Sugden is prepared to allow. Wesley does stipulate that the righteousness thereby defined is "inward righteousness," whereas the second commandment related to "outward righteousness." If only the latter is considered ethics proper, then Sugden's critique may have some merit, but that fails to see the holistic vision of the Wesleyan view of the Christian life as entailing both inward being and outward behaving.

Taken together these two commandments constitute holiness of heart and life, and, Wesley emphasizes, this holiness is happiness or "holistic well-being" or shalom in its fullest significance. This is "true religion."[4]

In his first sermon on the Sermon on the Mount, Wesley defines righteousness as "the life of God in the soul; the mind which was in Christ Jesus; the image of God stamped upon the heart, now renewed after the likeness of Him that created it," and asks, "What is it but the love of God, because He first loved us, and the love of all mankind for His sake."[5]

Wesley consistently recognized that "love for God" is a response to God's love for us. Thus, while he does not address the issue, the meaning of agape in the first commandment cannot be identical to that in the second commandment. As Gene Outka says,

The fitting attitudes and actions toward the two objects may often differ patently. One is free to worship and obey God; but to worship the neighbor is an act of idolatry. And one may suffer and forgive the neighbor, but to presume to "forgive" God would constitute blasphemy.[6]

Love for God as Obedience

This raises a further question as to whether or not it is legitimate to include love for God as a normative ethical principle since God is the agent to which we respond. Kierkegaard's critique of the confusion involved with the term *love* in the two commandments does suggest a line of development that is ethical and turns out to be biblical.

A man must love God in *unconditional obedience* and love him in *adoration*. It would be ungodliness if any man dared love himself in this way, or dared love another person in this way, or dared let another person love him in this way.[7]

This statement points to the correlative relation between love for God and obedience to him. That truth is implicit in the Genesis saga of the pre-Fall Garden relation. The condition for this relation of communion was obedience, but a very important ethical consideration is that obedience in the abstract is existentially meaningless. Consequently the Lord did not give the contentless command "Your probation is conditioned on your obedience." He identified a specific point of obedience: "You may freely eat of every tree of the garden; but you must not eat from the tree of the knowledge of good and evil" (Gen 2:16-17).

The prophet who thinks he or she is proclaiming a radical message by vigorously calling the congregation to obedience to the will of God will neither arouse any opposition nor create any change of behavior. Every sincere professing Christian believes that whatever he or she is doing is in obedience to God, and thus the message has no application to him or her. For a clear illustration of a proper proclamation of obedience to God's will, read the classical Old Testament prophets, notably Isaiah, Amos, Hosea and Micah. They became very specific about what both obedience and disobedience entailed.

Obedience was the key to maintaining the relationship to God that was the central component of the image of God. The tragic story of Genesis depicts how this relation was disrupted and distorted, resulting in the first pair being driven from the Garden and from communion with the Creator. The narrative points out the impossibility of human's returning to the Garden on their own initiative by describing the Lord placing a flaming sword at the entrance to guard against a return on the wrong basis (Gen 3:24). But this only highlights the priority of grace in the divine-human relation. The Lord himself begins immediately to make overtures to his fallen creation and to take steps to restore what was lost in the Fall.

Thus, as noted earlier in this study, by a sheer act of grace God moved to effect a deliverance from the bondage of sin for those who would avail themselves of his offer of salvation. For those who responded and were translated from the kingdom of darkness into the kingdom of God, the Lord offers a developing relationship that moves in the direction of a renewal of the image, that is, a full relation to him.

Obedience as Teleological

As we explore obedience as the ethical implication of this relation, it appears on the surface that we are building a case for an ethic of legalism that makes obedience an end in itself. But this is not so when we recognize that obedience to the law is not an end in itself but a means to an end, teleological in nature. Jesus' condemnation of the rigorous legal righteousness of the Pharisees makes this abundantly clear.

The end of obedience is communion, not obedience. So merely observing the letter of the law is not an adequate means of maintaining and developing a relation of communion. First John 3:22 captures this perspective: "We obey his commands and do what pleases him."

Deuteronomy speaks of a close correlation between love and obedience (cf. 6:4-5; 7:9). This theme becomes very explicit in the Gospel of John but is interpreted there in relation to Jesus and is closely tied to belief in him. Jesus said to his disciples, "If you love me, you will obey what I command" (14:15). This is also tied in with the promised gift of the Holy Spirit.

While the relation between God and his people is legitimately seen as Sovereign and subject, the New Testament makes much more of the relation, putting it in terms of Father and child. The ideal relation between parent and child is not simply authority and submission, with the parent imposing rules and the child obeying merely out of a desire for acceptance or fear of punishment. The ideal is love, where the parent is given oversight for the well-being of the child, who recognizes this and responds because of mutual love, trust and respect. While this ideal may seldom be found within human families, there is no reason why it cannot exist between our heavenly Father and those who experience an "Abba Father" relationship.

I suggest two very practical implications of this relationship for living out the image of God. First, it provides us with a principle of discrimination concerning which aspects of life should be avoided and which embraced. Paul suggests this when he says in Colossians 3:15, "Let the peace of Christ rule in your hearts." The word translated in the RSV as "rule" carries the meaning of "arbitrate" or "umpire." The umpire is the one who calls fouls, out of bounds and other infractions of the rules of the game. How does the peace of Christ do this? In the sense that anything that disturbs that "peace," that relation of communion with God, should be avoided in the Christian life. It can be compared to the reflection of one's face in a pool of still water. When a pebble is dropped into the pool, it distorts the reflection. Anything that distorts or dims the face of our Father should be whistled "out of bounds."

British holiness writer Thomas Cook has suggested a number of analogies to emphasize the guidance of this principle. He compares it to the test-flame that would be lowered into a mine shaft to test the oxygen level. If the flame flickered or was extinguished, it was determined that the shaft was too dangerous for human life. Or it is like a compass to a sailor when the stars are obscured and no landmarks can be seen. Christ's peace immediately shrinks in the presence of an evil thing. There is nothing more precious that we would exchange the peace of Christ for.

This is the same principle that informs the famous definition of sin proposed by Susannah Wesley, the mother of John and Charles: "Whatever weakens your reason, impairs the tenderness of your conscience, obscures your sense of God, or takes off the relish of spiritual things, whatever increases the authority of your body over mind, that thing for you is sin."[8]

Here we have a much more sensitive guideline than legalistic rules, even though it does involve a measure of subjectivity. But that element of subjectivity can be sensitized against perversion by constant attention to the character of Christ, who is the model of this unruffled peace based on his relation of oneness with the Father.

Love for God—A Principle of Separation

The second ethical implication of this relationship for living out the image of God is that it provides us with a principle of separation. Many people in the late-nineteenth- and early-twentieth-century revivalistic movement had a firm grasp on the necessity of separation. The problem was that too many did not base their emphasis on a theological principle, and therefore much of their ethical emphasis was defined by the contemporary culture. A survey of the history of this movement places its adherents among what secular historians call "custodians of culture." With the emerging wealth and accompanying secular lifestyles of the time that influenced the "old-line churches," these people were, to a great extent, seeking to perpetuate a set of cultural mores that had been generally accepted in the polite society of an earlier period. Many simply called for total separation from society per se. There were few entertainments that were not off limits. Virtually no activity was permitted among some groups except purely religious ones.[9]

My suggested principle of separation would say something like this: Since in my relationship with God I acknowledge him as absolute sovereign and loving Father, any activity that compromises that relation must be avoided. This has the advantage of being a theological rather than a sociological principle.

Many of the prohibitions found in the "holiness code" in the Old Testament can be based on this principle. A simple reading of these instructions concludes that they are essentially dietary. While there are certain dietary features that have a direct relation to physical well-being, the repeated refrain attached to them, "I am the LORD [Yahweh]," suggests a more theologically oriented reason. One major reason certain foods are excluded from the Hebrew "grocery list" may be that they had some connection with pagan worship.[10]

An aspect of the early Christian lifestyle illustrates this principle. Many avoided athletic games in the amphitheater because they were conducted in honor of pagan gods. To participate would have been to compromise their exclusive loyalty to the one true and living God. Most games would likely not be sinful in and of themselves, although certain ones would be unacceptable to the Christian conscience, such as gladiators fighting to the death. The theological principle of divine sovereignty served as the determining principle. The Christian must avoid whatever compromises that sovereignty, which would include activity dedicated to pagan deities. This was one basis for a widespread Christian opposition during the early part of this century to the lodge, or secret orders, where the name of Jesus could not be mentioned.

Jesus himself provides us with a model of this principle of separation in contrast to the self-righteousness of the Pharisees. His association with those persons the Pharisees avoided was for redemptive purposes, since, as he put it, "It is not the healthy who need a doctor, but the sick" (Luke 5:31). He controlled the ethos and was not dominated by the sinful aspect of their lives.

If we put this in the context of mission, which is the raison d'être of the church, we can capture the importance of avoiding any lifestyle that compromises the lordship of Christ. To yield to the temptation of acknowledging the priority of worldly values would militate against the witness of the one who professes to love God with undivided love.

Eight

THE IMAGE AS RELATION TO OTHERS

If the first relation that constitutes the *imago Dei* was difficult to ascertain from the Genesis creation narratives, the second is abundantly explicit. And, as we will see, its ethical implications are repeatedly spelled out in the rest of Scripture as well.

Humanity as Social—Biblical Basis

Genesis 1:26 presents us with an unusual phenomenon. The creation story in the Hebrew scripture, in contrast to similar creation accounts from the ancient world, is self-consciously monotheistic. Therefore it comes as quite a surprise to see the use of plural pronouns: "Let *us* make man in *our* image, in *our* likeness." This emphasis is spelled out further in the fact that humankind is created male and female. And the Hebrew word used for God in 1:1 is *Elohim,* the plural of *El,* the generic Hebrew name for "God." What is the meaning of all this?

Some scholars say that the plural reference is to a divine court, a collection of lesser beings gathered around God. This seems to have some support in a few other passages. But theologically it is more sound to look in another direction. Some popular Bible teachers suggest that here we have an Old Testament reference to the Trinity, a New Testament truth. This is anachronistic. I believe the best way to explain these references that suggest a plurality in God is to interpret them to mean that God has a social nature, interpersonal in character.[1] The implication of this for the meaning of the *imago Dei* is clear. In the words of Philip E. Hughes, "The Creator of man as male and female, together with the encouragement to 'be fruitful and multiply,' shows that man was intended to be a communal being enjoying personal fellowship with his fellow humans."[2]

The nature of the relationship between people that the Creator intended is symbolized by the first pair's pre-Fall unashamed nakedness. That this has spiritual (and ethical) overtones is emphasized when they felt shame and covered themselves immediately upon assuming lordship of their own lives. This suggests that the divinely intended nature of interpersonal relations was openness and freedom marked by the absence of a self-centered dimension that would use another person for one's own ends.

The remainder of Genesis 1—11 contains several pictures of distorted relationships that resulted from the Fall. The conflict between Cain and Abel depicted the most disastrous consequence of interpersonal estrangement. The climactic story is the incident of the tower of Babel, which resulted in the confusion of languages and the dispersion of people from each other. Even the superficial reader of Scripture will note that community is an essential feature of God's redemptive intention as he sets about to reverse and correct the consequences of the Fall. Pentecost became the New Testament paradigm of this intention.

Neighbor Love as an Ethical Principle

When God set out to redeem and restore his fallen creation he intended to renew people's relations not only to him but also to each other. This introduces the most overtly expressed and demonstrated ethical principle in Scripture: we are to "love our neighbor as ourselves" (Lev 19:18; Mt 5:43-48; Mk 12:28-34; Lk 6:22-36). Wesley insisted on this as one of the two branches of true religion. Many of the ethical decisions we make pertain to the practical living out of this command. Even the most superficial understanding of this ideal recognizes that it also raises some of the most thorny issues of the moral life.

For example, if God's ideal for interpersonal relation is openness to each other, to what extent is this possible under the conditions of existence? In what context is it to be manifested? To what degree are we to be open and possibly make ourselves vulnerable to abuse and misuse? These questions never arise when we are thinking about our relation to God. But we are living in a world of human beings who are fallen, and this introduces another dimension.

It is helpful to recognize the possibility of different degrees of openness in different contexts. The most intimate relationship between two people is an ideal marriage. It is no doubt for this reason that the relationship between God and his people, or between Christ and the church, is often illustrated by the husband-wife analogy. This might be a clue to what is implied in the creation narratives: that God's intended relation between male and female be monogamous. The radical openness that can exist between two persons who are unequivocally committed to each other with no competing loves or loyalties is impossible in polygamous or polyandrous relations. Of course if there is irrational jealousy or lack of trust in a monogamous relationship, it can never be completely open. Mutuality and reciprocity are essential components of the ideal relationship.

This analogy can be expanded to include the family and the community of faith. But with each expansion there is an increasing lack of freedom to be radically open. Theoretically in the church there should be uninhibited freedom to be open about our inner and outer lives, but in our fallen condition each of us will likely feel a certain inhibition, even with those who are among the saints. Paul recognized the difficulties inherent in the present state as he advised: "If it is possible, as far as it depends on you, live at peace with everyone" (Rom 12:18). Outside the community of faith significant obstacles are present, and only rarely, if ever, can this radical openness exist.[3]

The practical reality of this situation once again highlights the incompleteness of our ethical perfection. An ideal for the community of faith is set before us, but its actualization is eschatological, that is, it awaits the glorification of the church. Note the eschatological dimension of Ephesians 5:24-27: "Christ loved the church and gave himself up for her to make her holy, cleansing her by the washing with water through the word, and to present her to himself as a radiant church, without stain or wrinkle or any other blemish, but holy and blameless."

Love for God and Others Is Inseparable

Despite the difficulties that arise when we attempt to apply this ideal, our relation to God and our relation to fellow human beings is inseparable. The author of Hebrews emphasizes this inseparable connection in 12:14: "Make every effort to live in peace with all men and to be holy; without holiness no one will see the Lord." Unfortunately this text has too frequently been dissected. The last part is taken seriously but the first part is ignored. We do this to our peril.

When the Gospel writers report Jesus' conversations about the "first" or "greatest" commandment, both vertical and horizontal aspects are included. The context makes it clear that these two relationships are inseparable from each other.

The central way that the Bible, as well as Wesley, speaks about our ethical relation to others is in terms of love. All three synoptic Gospels show Jesus either stating or approving that love of God and love of neighbor is the essence of the law. This is not a creation out of whole cloth but a pulling together of two passages found in the Torah: Deuteronomy 6:4-5 declares, "Love the LORD your God with all your heart and with all your soul and with all your strength," and Leviticus 19:18 commands, "Love your neighbor as yourself. I am the LORD."

Both Matthew (5:43-48) and Luke (6:27-36) expand the second commandment to include love of enemies. In the Sermon on the Mount, Jesus contrasts this "higher righteousness" with that of the scribes and Pharisees. It is true that nowhere does the Old Testament say to hate your enemies, but New Testament scholars argue that this was the natural interpretation based on silence that was prevalent in first-century rabbinic teaching.[4]

When Jesus gave the model prayer to his disciples, it included the petition "Forgive us our trespasses [debts, sins] as we forgive those who trespass against us." It is significant that this is the only petition on which Jesus commented. In doing so he reinforced its centrality by saying that it is impossible to be rightly related to God without being rightly related to our brother or sister, and by implication, our "enemy."

This is the thrust of being perfect as the Father in heaven is perfect (Mt 5:48). To understand the ethical implications of this we must explore intensively the love commandment.

Swedish bishop and theologian Gustaf Aulén, who vigorously opposed Nazi influence in his country, gives an excellent summary of the love commands.

"Loving God" means primarily . . . obeying the will of God. "Loving one's neighbor" means neither infatuation nor sentimental compassion, but above all a caring and an attentiveness which expresses itself in practical deed, whose basis is men's open hearts toward one another and toward the demands for a life together. The decisive thing was that God's ethical demands were to be fulfilled within the human community.[5]

The Problem of Neighbor

What does it mean to "love our neighbor as ourselves"? Perhaps the best answer to this question is found in Jesus' response to the lawyer's question, "Who is my neighbor?" It was an academic question (Lk 10:29-37). Jesus responded by telling the parable of the good Samaritan.

This familiar parable has a triple whammy. In the first place, it puts into focus the qualifier to neighbor love, "as you love yourself." If you identify yourself with the wounded man by the roadside, it becomes immediately apparent what you would desire another to do on your behalf. The story indirectly throws light on the so-called golden rule, "Do to others as you would have them do to you" (Lk 6:31).

It is important to note that this is not a command to love oneself. Some have seen it this way, but many Christian ethicists have argued that it is disastrous to introduce self-love onto the ground floor of a Christian ethical understanding.[6] We do this naturally, and it comes very close to the soundest definition of the nature of sin. Rather, "as you would have them do to you" becomes a criterion for when one should apply the principle of neighbor love. "The point is that the neighbor must be no less an object of our loving concern than our own life inevitably is."[7] We will see the importance of this "need-orientation" shortly.

Second, the characters in the parable illuminate the "higher righteousness" of Jesus' ethic by having the Samaritan help the Jew. Samaritans were despised by the Jews, so it would have come as quite a shock to a first-century Jew to hear this story. He would immediately recognize that Jesus was saying that love for neighbor transcends all natural boundaries, even those created by race and religion.

Third, and possibly the most significant, is the way in which Jesus responded to the lawyer's question, "Who is my neighbor?" What is startling is that Jesus did not answer that question, but another, "To whom should I be a neighbor?" This becomes clear when Jesus puts this question to the questioner at the conclusion of the discourse.

Several results follow from this subtle shift. The question was abstract, academic. Jesus moves it into the practical realm and turns it into an existential question. As Victor Paul Furnish said, "Thus, the problem of 'neighbor' is not one of definition but of performance, and where there is performance, where one's deeds are moved and shaped by love, there is neither time nor reason to ask, *who* is my neighbor?"[8]

Perhaps the most significant implication of shifting the question is that to have answered the question literally and strictly would have opened the door to a limitation of love. In typical rabbinic fashion the lawyer wanted a precise definition. But if *neighbor* could have been defined in this way, it would have been possible to identify some people who did not conform to the definition. In other words, it would have become an exclusive concept, whereas the love enjoined by Jesus was inclusive. It embraced all who needed him and to whom he was capable of ministering.

The Nature of Love for the Other Person

Discussions about the Christian's relation to others have characteristically revolved around the meaning of *agapē*. *Agapē* is the distinctive Greek word used in the New Testament for God's kind of love that is to be manifested by the believer toward others. It is often contrasted with other Greek words that have emotional content and are based on a quality in the one who is loved that meets a need in the one who loves. Agape, on the other hand, is an other-regarding attitude and behavior that is independent of the loveliness of the other person. It seeks his or her well-being even though there is no benefit derived by the believer.

William Barclay, among others, argues that agape is not based on any emotional feeling toward another but is best expressed as "good will."[9] On this basis it is possible to command neighbor love, since a feeling cannot be commanded. Others think this is too restrictive of the actual use of the term in the New Testament. Kierkegaard contrasts the love that is commanded with "immediate love," which is the love of impulse and inclination. The love that is commanded, he argued, is grounded in eternity and is thus unchangeable.[10]

We do not have to settle these issues to recognize that agape love is the divine ideal for our relation to others. And it certainly carries the connotation of seeking the well-being of our neighbor as we do our own. But this raises some serious ethical questions: To what degree are we to allow our neighbor to determine his or her own need? Are we to treat all persons alike, or do we have regard for their individual situation? Does agape distinguish between the other's needs and allowing that other to exploit me in order to satisfy his or her perceived needs or desires?

Even some of Jesus' descriptions of "other-relation" in the Sermon on the Mount raises these questions. As many have pointed out, if we indiscriminately follow his instructions to "give to the one who asks you, and do not turn away from the one who wants to borrow from you" (Mt 5:42), we may be doing more harm to that person than good. The question is, how does one love with discrimination yet without partiality?

A possible answer to these difficult questions may be found in the concept of "need." This, we saw, emerged as a definitive concept out of the parable of the good Samaritan. A related insight has become popular among those who deal with a friend's or family member's addiction. To indiscriminately support their habit by "bailing them out" and covering for them is to become codependent. The most redemptive answer is to manifest "tough love." Their need is to come face to face with their problem and thus be more likely to seek help. If we can contribute to this outcome by withholding aid, by allowing them to experience the consequences of their addiction, as painful as it may be, we are really showing agape love. If, on the other hand, we continue providing them with the support to satisfy their own perceived needs, we do them a disastrous disservice.

Kierkegaard is certainly correct when he says,

If your beloved or your friend begged you for something which you, because you honestly loved him, had anxiously considered would be injurious to him: then a responsibility would rest upon you if you showed your love by acquiescing in his wish, instead of showing it by denying him its fulfillment. . . . If you can better perceive his best than he can, then you will not be able to excuse yourself by the fact that the harmful thing was his own wish, was what he himself asked for. . . . But this you simply have no right to do; you are responsible if you do it, just as the other is responsible if he should misuse his relationship to you in this way.[11]

In a somewhat different vein John Wesley recognized the validity of being discriminate when distributing one's possessions. He advises to distribute possessions first to those for whom you have primary responsibility, your own family; then, as you have resources available, to the household of faith, and if still available, to others.[12] This is a calculating love that clearly provides a rather commonsense criterion for living out the ethic of love. It might easily be perverted, but it has much to commend it.

Now to return to our basic point of reference: our renewal in the divine image. If it was God's creative intention to bring into being a body of persons who would exist in a relation of openness, one in which all persons were recognized as having intrinsic worth and treated in that light, then this is also his redemptive goal. If we are truly reflecting the divine image in interpersonal relations, we can never turn other persons into things to be used for our own self-centered ends. We cannot treat them as an "it."

Love and the Male-Female Relation

This principle finds its most graphic application in the relation between man and woman. While sexual attraction is not the consequence of the Fall, as some have mistakenly taught, the Fall did introduce an element into sexual relations that tends to warp those attractions into lust, which becomes the basis for exploitation of the other person. It is this principle that makes sexual relations outside of marriage a violation of God's design. A total life commitment is the essence of marriage, and it seems impossible to merely cohabit on any other basis than self-gratification.

This aspect of our theological principle also addresses the issue of modesty. While this has become a subject on which few dare to speak today, it is important and is a subject taken up by Scripture (see 1 Tim 2:9; 1 Pet 3:3-5). These passages do not condemn adornment in toto but suggest that natural beauty, what one really is, is the proper basis for a relationship. Dressing to inappropriately entice the opposite sex or to create a false illusion about beauty is questionable in the light of the image of God.

H. Orton Wiley's words are wise: "We may say then that the Christian should dress in a manner that will not attract undue attention either by expensive apparel or eccentric plainness; and that will leave upon your observers, the impression of the wearer as being of a meek and quiet spirit."[13]

Other-Relations and Mission

Guidelines for Israel's lifestyle are replete with instructions concerning other-relations within the community of faith. The judges were given specific instructions regarding equal treatment of all persons: "Do not show partiality in judging; hear both small and great alike. Do not be afraid of any man, for judgment belongs to God" (Deut 1:17).

In particular those people who were without clout, who were at the mercy of the world, were to be especially cared for. The widow, the orphan and the noncitizen were repeatedly mentioned as special objects of concern by other members of the community.

We saw earlier that the ideal for the people of God was embodied in the word *shalom*. The prophets emphasized the other-relation aspect of shalom in particular. According to the true prophet, the false prophet cried, " 'Shalom, shalom,' they say, when there is no shalom" (Jer 8:11). There was no war, prosperity reigned within the nation, and on the surface things seemed great. But, said the true prophet, the rich are oppressing the poor, who cannot find justice in the law courts. These inequities invalidate the claim that there is shalom.

When we turn to the New Testament we find a similar emphasis concerning the life of the church. Beginning with Acts, one of the central concerns of the biblical writers is the unity of the church. The unity of the church (an ideal that apparently existed only for a short time after Pentecost) was the characteristic that made the greatest impact on those outside. The overarching theme of the high priestly prayer of our Lord was mission. And the unity of his followers was the centerpiece to carrying out that mission (Jn 17).

It is easy to see how the absence of unity among those who profess the name of Christ hampers their mission. And it is easy to see how the outsider is unimpressed by "Christians" who are constantly squabbling with each other. If holiness of heart and life will do anything for us, it will eliminate the spirit of dissension and promote a peaceable spirit. Holiness is shalom.

In light of the concepts developed in this chapter, one can see how the idea of the people of God—the church—should be understood as the embodiment of God's redemptive intention in the world. It is here that the divine intention purposes to call into being a people who actualize the ideal of this other-relation, which constitutes the renewal of people in the divine image. This raises such large and significant ethical issues that their development calls for a separate chapter.

Nine

THE CHURCH AS CONTEXT FOR CHRISTIAN ETHICS

Many things have contributed to our present religious individualism that militates against a biblical understanding of the church (ecclesiology). Noted scientist and philosopher Alfred North Whitehead's definition of religion as "what the individual does with his own solitariness" has been generally embraced by the average Christian in Western culture, but without the philosophical sophistication of Whitehead's understanding. This emphasis on religious individualism is generally accompanied by a purely personal approach to morality.

Corporate Nature of Biblical Faith

John Wesley would have none of this, as is reflected in his oft-quoted statements that there is no such thing as an "individual Christian" and "no holiness but social holiness." Modern theologians concur with this. In fact some have been speaking about a "rediscovery of the church" in the twentieth century.[1] But as David H. C. Read has observed, this recovery has been pretty well insulated within academic theological circles.

The Church and its theologians may have moved far from an individualistic understanding of the Gospel, and the clergy may preach themselves hoarse on the subject of our corporate moral engagement and responsibility, but the average citizen of the Protestant western world is still inclined to think that Christian ethics is a matter for the private conscience.[2]

Christian ethics is a response to the gracious activity of God. The point that must be stressed here is that from the Christian point of view, "ethical analysis cannot begin with or be based upon human insights, ideas, or attitudes, for all of these are distorted; rather, it must have its basis in and through what happens in God's act."[3] *And what God does in his redemptive act is call a community of faith into existence.*

The solidarity of the people of God under the old covenant is easily recognized, but many fail to see that this same solidarity is present under the new. The best New Testament scholarship agrees that Jesus' intention was to establish a new people of God, and this was overtly symbolized by his choice of the Twelve, an obvious indication of continuity with the old Israel. The contrast is not between group and individual but between a body chiefly identified by racial boundaries and one that knew no such restrictions.[4]

The church as understood in the New Testament is brought into being by the Holy Spirit, and that reception (or bestowal) constitutes one part of the koinonia of the Spirit. People do not join the church as they would an organization that was created by its members; people become a part of the family by their new birth into Christ's church, which was created by him. It is fascinating that in the book of Acts, where we have a picture of the pristine church, individuals do not receive the Spirit; only the group does. Paul's experience is no exception, since he receives the Spirit only when the church, in the person of Ananias, comes and lays hands on him.

This corporate understanding of the church in relation to the indwelling Holy Spirit is present throughout the writings of Paul. In accord with the portrait drawn in Acts of the church as a Spirit-constituted body, he describes the church as the temple of the Holy Spirit. In a passage fraught with ethical overtones, Paul says to the Corinthians, "Don't you know that you yourselves are God's temple and that God's Spirit lives in you? If anyone destroys God's temple, God will destroy him; for God's temple is sacred, and you are that temple" (1 Cor 3:16-17). Paul uses these same words later to describe the individual, but the two are correlative and inseparable concepts.

Authentic Versus Inauthentic Corporate Life

The corporate life of the church is an important source of ethical wisdom, and this clearly sets up a tension with the widespread mood of individualism. Thus it is not surprising that resistance is the normal reaction to a call for corporate existence. This resistance is an appropriate response to the conformity that submerges an individual's unique personality and legitimate freedom. And unfortunately there is significant justification for this concern in light of the many cases of spiritual abuse by leaders with a messiah complex. One need only think about the Jim Jones tragedy or David Koresh's followers at Waco and more recent events in Canada and Europe. Numerous but less graphic types of such abuse occur in the church more frequently than we might be aware. But when this is present it does not—and cannot—reflect true community, true koinonia.

Genuine community is found only in a relationship where each personality is respected, where no one person tries to dominate anyone else, where each person can speak freely, where each feels that the truth spoken by another person is uttered in respect and love and not for any impure motive. Genuine community is a relationship of harmony and peace, mutual trust and respect.

Such a condition could exist where each person involved lived out the servant role that is the calling of followers of Christ. This is the true authority and greatness that Jesus sought to inculcate in his followers, but they were slow to learn. Unfortunately we are too. The disciples argued over who would be the greatest in the kingdom, and Jesus responded by wrapping a towel around his waist—a symbol of service at the lowest level—and humbling them over their worldly standards of authority.

The rulers of this world lord it over their subjects, Jesus told them. But it is not to be so with those who are his disciples. Even the Lord himself came not to be ministered to but to minister and give his life as a ransom for many (Mk 10:45).

The ministry of Jesus is patterned after the servant of the Lord who is graphically pictured in Isaiah 53. Those who share his life are to be the servant-people. It is obvious that having such a heart would make it impossible for one person to impose in an authoritarian way on another person in order to destroy his or her individuality.

The church is ideally a community of agape. A fellowship built on this kind of love is not one in which one person is drawn to another because the latter meets a need of the former—eros love. Agape is a concern for the well-being of the other person, growing out of the love of God that was shed in the hearts of those who follow Christ (Rom 5:5). Thus this defining characteristic of koinonia stands as an additional safeguard against exploitation of an individual by a group or an ecclesiastical official.

Realistically, however, this describes an ideal church that probably doesn't exist as an empirical reality. It is a sad fact of life that all human actions fall short of perfection. However, here we encounter another ethical principle. One's ethical obligation is to strive for the ideal, not to acquiesce in the face of a general deviation from the good. No situation can ever improve unless those who are committed seek to realize the good in their own lives; to the extent that they do there is an increasing corporate conformity to the ideal. Though the empirical church will never be the eschatological church, short of the heavenly city, by the grace of God we need to become as free from "spot and wrinkle" as possible under our earthly conditions.

Church as Theonomous Community

The upshot of this is that authoritarianism—dominating people so that their individuality is thwarted and unfulfilled—is excluded from the church context. When the Spirit of God does his proper work of bringing his people's lives into conformity with the pattern set by Jesus Christ, each individual is treated with respect, and his or her dignity is never transgressed.

This truth can be further illuminated by a set of concepts first introduced by eighteenth-century philosopher Immanuel Kant and developed theologically by Paul Tillich: *autonomy, heteronomy* and *theonomy.* All are combinations of *nomos,* meaning "law," and a qualifying prefix. With the prefix *autos* the word means self-legislated law; with *heteros,* other-legislated law; and with *theos,* God-legislated law.

Kant, a proponent of the Enlightenment, insisted that the dignity of rational human beings is violated unless the law by which they live is *autos,* or self-imposed. Consequently he rejected both heteronomy and theonomy, thinking both are alien to people. The Enlightenment's declaration of independence from tradition and institutionalism was a valid reaction against an oppressive heteronomous situation, but the reaction went too far in the opposite direction.

Tillich seeks to rehabilitate these concepts in relation to his interpretation of revelation. He wants to retain the autonomy of human reason and still recognize that finite reason points beyond its own finitude to the "depth of reason." This reflects his concern to reject the idea that revelation comes to reason as a foreign or alien element that shatters the structures of reason. In that case it would be heteronomous.[5]

Nonetheless, unless revelation involves the impingement of that which is "beyond" our own reason, it would merely be humanistic discovery. Thus autonomy and heteronomy move against each other under the conditions of existence. Tillich's solution to this conflict is to see revelation as theonomous, that the "ground of being" (God) to which revelation bears witness is the "depth of reason" to which finite reason points. Thus when God manifests himself (revelation) reason is united with its own depth, or its own deepest significance, and consequently finds fulfillment and meaning, not destruction, as would be the case if God were not the ground of rationality. Autonomy is not lost and true heteronomy is retained; both find their resolution, at least partially, in theonomy.

These rather technical and perhaps difficult concepts point to an insight regarding ethics, the field Kant was primarily concerned with. Using Tillich's analysis we can extrapolate his insights into an ethical situation. The "law" of the Christian life, while coming from beyond, does not violate one's individuality and self-determination in any absolute sense so as to destroy one's autonomy, but rather enables the free individual to find that lifestyle which is the most fulfilling for his or her deepest nature. This is because humankind is essentially related to God *(imago Dei)* and becomes fully human only when the existential estrangement from God is overcome in grace. Simply put, God's commandments are not destructive of personhood but rather bring it to its highest realization. The psalmist realized this and exclaimed, "Great peace have they who love your law, and nothing can make them stumble" (Ps 119:165). Paul expresses the same theme in Romans 12:2: "Don't copy the behavior and customs of this world, but be a new and different person with a fresh newness in all you do and think. Then you will learn from your own experience how his ways will really satisfy you" (LB).

The church is ideally the fellowship of those who are open to the "ground of being" and who understand the ethical situation in a theonomous way. In love it can never elevate itself to a heteronomous authority, asserting itself destructively over the individual, but can only share its own insights regarding that which truly fulfills human personhood; conversely, it cannot tolerate irresponsible individualism that allows a person to choose a self-destructive path simply in order to allow self-determination. In a word, when the church is the church, it fosters the theonomous relationship to Christian ethics.

Tillich addresses the situation in a brief but insightful paragraph.

The church as the community of the New Being is the place where the new theonomy is actual. But from there it pours into the whole of man's cultural life and gives a Spiritual center to man's spiritual life. In the church as it should be, nothing is heteronomous in contrast to autonomous. And in man's spiritual life nothing is autonomous, in contrast to heteronomous, whenever spiritual life has an ultimate integration. But he further recognizes the distinction between the empirical church and the eschatological church (while not using these terms) and qualifies the "ideal" picture by observing,

> Yet this is not the human situation. The church is not only the community of the New Being; it is also a sociological group immersed in the conflicts of existence. Therefore, it is subject to the almost irresistible temptation of becoming heteronomous and of suppressing autonomous criticism, eliciting just by this method autonomous reactions which often are strong enough to secularize not only culture but also the church itself. A heteronomous tide may then start the vicious circle again. *But the church is never completely bereft of theonomous forces.*[6]

The danger of authoritarianism is always with us in corporate life. It must be guarded against, and when it appears it must be resisted in the name of the Lord. On the other side, with no less of a reprehensible character, is the perversion of irresponsible individualism. Here one ignores corporate responsibilities and the essential ties with the people of God in order to "do his own thing." It may be, and usually is, as much a violation of agape as authoritarianism is.

The Conscience of the Church

A further corollary of the church as context for ethical decision-making is the concept of the "conscience" of the church. This suggests a general consensus of those believers who compose the body of Christ or the part of it with which they are identified.

There are two ways the idea of the conscience of the church can be described. One is hierarchical (or authoritarian), and the other is congregational. How one envisions it is directly related to one's doctrine of the church.

An episcopal understanding naturally results in a hierarchical interpretation. Whether one sees the bishop as being the embodiment of the church or as having authority through apostolic succession, or even as possessing a lordly role toward the flock by acquiring the office through election, the result is the same. Because of inherent authority the hierarchy has both the right and the responsibility to impose the conscience of the church on the laity, whose obligation it is to obey without question. However, in such a situation it is really the conscience of the hierarchy that is being imposed on the "underlings," who are thereby reduced to second-class citizens in the church. The classic representative of this type of perspective is the old Roman Catholic Church. But it has also appeared all too frequently in Protestantism.

The view of the church that takes seriously the universal priesthood of believers and defines the church more broadly than ancient Catholicism takes the congregational approach, especially if it understands its nature. Here the distinction between people in the church, such as clergy and laypeople, is recognized as a functional difference only. Authority is something that is granted and exercised only by permission, and must be earned. The whole body is vested with equal authority in relation to each part, and if for various reasons it chooses to delegate that authority, the result is merely representational and not hierarchical.

On the basis of our earlier discussions of the nature of the church, we must conclude that only the second approach has any legitimacy. But even in this context, can we legitimately speak of the conscience of the church? Does it have any validity within the context of Christian ethics?

Before addressing these questions directly we should recall the nature of conscience discussed earlier in this book (see chapter two). The most important point to remember is that the content of conscience is learned as the result of many experiences. With this understanding in mind it makes sense to see the conscience of the church as the result of the collective experience of the body of Christ. There are two very important considerations to take into account in attempting to understand and apply this idea.

The first point to note is that when people are converted to the Christian faith they often bring with them a background of cultural experience that is less than Christian, if not anti-Christian. Such people certainly need the ethical nurture of the community of faith to guide their response to the grace that has changed their relationship to God. It is naive to suggest that these new believers' spiritual education should be left just to the Holy Spirit. As mentioned earlier, the Spirit works through the church. In Paul's letters are several examples of rudimentary ethical guidance he gives to new converts who are coming from a pagan environment, guidance that advanced Christians would see as elementary (e.g., 1 Cor 5:1-3; Col 3:7-9).

The second point to consider is that lone individuals are highly susceptible to surrounding influences and need the supporting conscience of the church for stability. No one would doubt that the Christian today is immersed in a sea of competing influences that pervert Christian values. A. T. Rasmussen describes the scene vividly:

> We live in a moral climate that surrounds us as pervasively as the air we breathe. We are bathed and saturated in it from the moment of our birth till the moment of our death. We breathe it into our lives as continuously and as unconsciously as the oxygen of the physical world. We develop our habits in the collective pattern of society called custom. Institutions organize the various aspects of our lives. Public opinion curtails our behavior and colors and tinctures our outlook. Even our consciences are never simon-pure but reflect the values under which we have developed.[7]

Elsewhere in his book Rasmussen speaks directly to the point emphasized here: "Lone individuals are easily intimidated or pressed into conformity by the temporary hysterias or band wagons of the world, unless they are bolstered and enlightened by the divine fellowship of inspiration and support. Much of this intimidation is both so subtle and so pervasive that it is never recognized."[8]

It is abundantly clear that when the nature of the church is expressed as a community of agape, of interdependent persons all striving to be conformed to the image of Christ (2 Cor 3:18), the experience of the church is an indispensable aid in understanding the character of the Christian lifestyle.

Identifying "The Church"

One last question remains to be explored: How is the church to be identified as the context in which the Christian ethic is lived out? Picture the individual standing in the center of three concentric circles. The largest circle, representing the most comprehensive context suggested by the idea of "the church," includes all people who have ever lived who have been grafted into the true vine, Jesus Christ. This includes Old Testament saints as well as all believers from the beginning of the Christian era. Those who have passed into the church triumphant are still part of the body of Christ, giving us access to the collective Christian wisdom of the ages.

The second concentric circle is the ecumenical church throughout the world, living and present. To appreciate this context we must avoid restricting the kingdom of God to our own group and recognize that God has his people everywhere, many of whom are different from us. This knowledge helps in properly responding to God's grace. It is all too easy to identify Christianity with certain cultural expressions. Failure to separate cultural mores from distinctly Christian moral norms can lead to a sanctification of class structures and cultural patterns that endangers the clear import of the Christian ethic. The only true New Testament church is an international church, and this calls for a perspective on ethics that transcends nationalistic ways of life.

The innermost circle of the church context is the particular religious group or denomination with which one identifies. Each denomination has its own commitments and distinctives that constitute its unique witness to the gospel. In order to maintain this witness each "church" has both the right and the obligation to spell out the kind of lifestyle that best expresses its uniqueness. This is the conscience of the church. And unless that lifestyle is the consensus of at least the overwhelming majority of the people in the church, it can be maintained only by a hierarchy. Such as result, as we have seen, betrays the nature of the church.

Ten

THE IMAGE AS RELATION TO THE EARTH

In the creation narrative humans are given "dominion" over the earth, a concept that is often misunderstood. Rather than a relation of exploitation that the term *dominion* seems to suggest, the real relation should be one of responsible stewardship. As the apex of God's creation, human beings are to care for the earth and use its resources for the glory of God, not for their own gratification.

As a result of the Fall the earth was cursed so that it resisted this responsible caretaking. But the responsibility was still there, although there were new elements that distorted the proper living out of this commission.

"The Land" in Old Testament Theology
The land was a central theological concept to Israel, appearing at the threshold of the story of God's redemptive activity in Genesis 12:1-3 and pervading the story to the very end of the Old Testament. How are we to understand this important concept? What are its ethical implications?

We must begin by understanding why God promised and eventually gave a piece of real estate to his chosen people. Few aspects of Scripture have been more misunderstood by evangelicals than this one, due to the influence of dispensational theology and the many "pop prophecy" books influenced by it. The best way to see its theological significance is to put the gift of the land in the context of the mission of Israel. They were given land in order to demonstrate in their use of it what God's creative intention was for humankind in relation to the earth. This is another piece of evidence that Israel was to be God's paradigm for the world.

Before exploring the ethical implications of this aspect of the *imago Dei* in the Old Testament, we need to place it in a larger picture. While the land is one of the most dominant themes in the Old Testament, references to it completely disappear in the New. If the land in terms of a specific piece of real estate and Israel's possession of it had an enduring place in God's redemptive plan for the world, wouldn't it be mentioned at least once by New Testament writers? But there is not the slightest whisper. Patrick D. Miller Jr. says on this point, "The promised land has lost its geographical character and the people of God are pilgrims and strangers on earth."[1]

What is one to make of this? It certainly suggests that from the New Testament perspective, contemporary evangelicals' preoccupation with the settlement of Jews on this particular piece of real estate is misguided. Hence we must look elsewhere for a more adequate explanation.

In light of the hermeneutical principle that the theological dimension is the enduring element of biblical faith, the theological role played by the land under the old covenant is now played by "possessions" in the new.[2] Thus the theological understanding that responsible stewardship of the land is central to Israel's mission is now transferred to possessions, all of which are the products of the earth (land). A careful reading of Jesus' ethical teaching shows this dominant concern. He says much about the subject.

Oswald Chambers quotes James Stalker, saying, "What He [Jesus] thought of most frequently as impeding the growth of true mankind was the pursuit of wealth and property." Chambers adds,

If we can save and do justly with money, we are absolutely certain we are right in the sight of God. . . . The two things around which our Lord centered His most scathing teaching were money and marriage, because they are the two things that make men and women devils or saints.[3]

Responsible Stewardship of the Land and Its Resources

We now turn to the ethical guidance of the Old Testament regarding how the people of God are to relate to the earth. There are two dimensions: One concerns the treatment of the land itself, what today we would call environmental ethics. The other pertains to the proper use of the land's produce. This impinges on what some refer to as "compassionate ministry." Both have enduring relevance for Christian ethics and must be given careful attention.

Two theological principles influence the ethical aspect of the land. First, the land is to be interpreted as a gift. This point is made by both narrative and proclamation. The stories of the conquest of Canaan leave little doubt that the success of this event was the result of divine intervention. Furthermore, God's word through his spokesmen made it clear that he had given them the land (Deut 5:31; 9:6; 11:17; 12:1; 17:7, 20; 26:9).

This emphasis is balanced by the repeated stress on the continued divine ownership (Lev 25:23; Ps 24:1). Thus Israel lives on the land as serfs or managers with Yahweh as the owner or lord, and their responsibility is to care for his property. The most overt recognition of their stewardship is the tithe of all the produce of the earth. This is a symbolic act testifying to their relationship to Yahweh as responsible stewards.

These two principles undergird the instructions for the care of the earth and the proper disposal of its fruits. Explicit provisions were made for good environmental policies. The land itself was not to be stripped of its fertility by uninterrupted sowing and reaping. Every seven years a field was to lie fallow to restore its strength. Trees were not to be cut wholesale from the forest. Clear-cutting, as we call it today, was forbidden.

These guidelines have enduring ethical significance. The responsible oversight of the environment is part of God's creative intention for the human race. Much attention has been given to this, especially since the 1960s, because of evidence that exploiting the earth for our own gratification is resulting in environmental deterioration that, if not checked, will eventually cause the annihilation of life on the earth. These concerns militate against a type of otherworldly spirituality that is so heavenly minded as to be of no earthly use. Holiness of heart and life is not a gnosticism that disparages the physical. Its resistance to worldliness has nothing to do with a lack of concern for the earth, the environment in which we live. Seen in terms of the holistic vision of biblical theology, recycling nonrenewal resources is being just as spiritual as attending a prayer meeting, although of course not a substitute.

The gift of the land makes provision for every family to own property, and this property is to be held in perpetuity. There was to be no permanent sale of land. It could always be redeemed, and every fifty years in the Year of Jubilee all land was to revert to its original owner. The purpose of this was to give security and make provision for all persons to live with a sense of dignity and self-esteem. Some of the prophets' most scathing condemnations were directed toward the perversion of these provisions.

Here we see how the closely related social and economic angles of Old Testament ethics come together. Landowners were not to glean their fields and were to leave the corners unharvested so that the poor could glean the grain freely. This supplied the poor with both sustenance and the dignity of work in gathering their own harvest.

Jesus' parable of the rich fool embodies this same ethical principle (Lk 12:16-21). Note the repeated use of the personal possessive pronoun in the monologue. The successful farmer failed to acknowledge the source of his success and assumed a false sense of ownership. He furthermore failed to understand the proper answer to his own question, "What shall I do with my goods?" The biblical answer would have been to use them to meet the needs of the less fortunate and destitute.

Patrick Miller, in his essay on the deuteronomic theology of the land, gives an excellent summary of the practical implications of this theology. The crucial question remains for us as for Israel: What shall we do with the land God gives? From the Christian perspective—and in the light of Deuteronomy—we are called to see that the enjoyment of the land and the use of its benefits are made available to all who dwell in it. What that means in terms of economic program and land use must be determined in very specific contexts, but because God had given the good gift we shall see that it is available to all. Because some—by God's blessing—shall benefit greatly from this gift, it is imperative that we see that provision for enjoyment of the land and its produce is made for the poor and the weak and the left out. Poverty, though a fact, is not desirable. Response to its presence in the land must not be passive acceptance but extra effort to care for the poor, to provide opportunity for all.[4]

John Wesley on Possessions

One of John Wesley's major concerns has to do with the proper distribution of possessions in alleviating human need. His principle is that "if you do not spend your money in doing good to others, you must spend it to the hurt of yourself."

If we waste our money, we are not only guilty of wasting a talent which God has given us, but we do ourselves the farther [sic] harm, we turn this useful talent into a powerful means of corrupting ourselves; because so far as it is spent wrong, so far it is spent in the support of some wrong temper, in gratifying some vain and unreasonable desires, which, as Christians, we are obliged to renounce.[5]

Almost everyone with a passing acquaintance with Wesley knows about his three rules regarding money. He refers to them in several of his sermons. Simply put, they are (1) make all you can, (2) save all you can and (3) give all you can. These three points provide the outline for his sermon "On the Use of Money."[6]

In each case he gives detailed guidance to living by these instructions, each rule having significant ethical implications. He stipulates that the first rule should be followed without hurting ourselves or our neighbor, and always within the bounds of honesty and legality.

The second rule does not mean to enlarge your bank account with surplus funds, although he recognized and approved of accumulating wealth consistent with "the carrying on our worldly business, in such a measure and degree" as is in accord with the overarching principle of doing all to the glory of God.[7] In fact, he freely admits that he inadvertently became rich.[8]

In elaborating the third point Wesley makes some prudential stipulations. He is clearly not arguing for either poverty or irresponsible dispensing of one's possessions. There are specific guidelines for "giving all you can."

If you desire to be "a faithful and wise steward," out of that portion of your Lord's goods which he has for the present lodged in your hands, but with the right of resumption whenever it pleaseth him, (1.) Provide things needful for yourself; food to eat, raiment to put on; whatever nature moderately requires, for preserving you both in health and strength. (2.) Provide these for your wife, your children, your servants, or any others who pertain to your household. If, when this is done, there is an overplus left, then do good to "them that are of the household of faith." If there be an overplus still, "as you have opportunity, do good unto all men." In so doing, you *give all you can;* nay, in a sound sense, all you have.[9]

In order to round out the discussion we need only add the note that how we as Christian disciples dispose of our possessions is a witness to our faith. If we spend all our wealth on our own self-gratification, beyond our needs, we testify to a set of values that are at best sub-Christian. And we certainly run the risk of believing that the meaning of life is to be found in the accumulation of things. In a word, our witness, or mission, is closely related to how we handle our possessions.

Eleven

THE IMAGE AS
RELATION TO SELF

T he relation to self is the determinative factor in the *imago Dei,* since a wrong estimate of self in relation to God, others and the earth is what constitutes a sinful relation. If self is elevated to the place of God in one's life, if self-centeredness is the determiner of how we relate to other people, if self-gratification is how we relate to possessions, then all of life is perverted. It then becomes the essence of what Paul refers to as "the flesh" *(sarx)*: the self seeking its own ends in independence from God.

The Dilemmas of Self-Love
Discussions on this subject usually revolve around the phrase that comes into view in connection with the command of neighbor-love, *as thyself.* We have touched on this briefly in our discussion of the *imago* as relation to the other, but now the issue returns for more careful and extensive consideration.

The question raised by *as thyself* introduces one of the most difficult and puzzling paradoxes in Christian ethics. On the one hand the classic definition of sin involves self-centeredness. On the other hand there is abundant evidence against a total self-denigration and certainly *for* the kind of teleological ethics that has happiness as its outcome, such as Wesleyan theology advocates. In light of the view that the essence of sin is self-love, it is proper to say, as Paul Ramsey does, that "no more disastrous mistake can be made than to admit self-love onto the ground floor of Christian ethics, as a basic part of Christian obligation."[1] This warning is actually directed against a long tradition, beginning with Augustine, that suggests the second commandment implicitly contains a third command to "love yourself."

But there is, as many psychologists argue, a natural self-love that is almost instinctual. This ineradicable principle in the normal human psyche seeks both survival and the good for the self. This much is assumed and becomes the point of reference in the command of neighbor-love. The words of Kierkegaard capture this position:

> Self-love is the underlying principle, or *the principle that is made to lie under,* in all love; whence if we conceive a religion of love, this religion need make but one assumption, as epigrammatic as true, and take its realization for granted: namely the condition that man loves himself, in order to command him to love his neighbor as himself.[2]

This stipulation, however, must be modified for Christian ethics by the reorientation known as the new birth, the beginning of sanctification or renewal in the *imago Dei.* This "real change" does not intend the eradication of the natural love of self but its distortion resulting from sin. Wesley notes in exploring the meaning of *meekness* in the Beatitudes that the meek "do not desire to extinguish any of the passions which God has for wise ends implanted in their nature; but they have the mastery of all: They hold them all in subjection, and employ them only in subservience to those ends."[3]

This transformation relocates the believer to a different sphere of existence described by Paul as "in Christ" or "in the Spirit." George F. Thomas properly contrasts the two spheres with regard to self-estimate: "The principle of life 'in the flesh' is love of self, aiming at the *satisfaction* of its own desires; the principle of life 'in the Spirit' is love of God and love of neighbor leading to the *transcendence* of the self."[4]

Wesley makes the same point in a different way by referring the love of neighbor to love of God by way of the cleansing of the heart, or inward transformation.

> It behooves us, therefore, to examine well upon what foundation our love of our neighbour stands; whether it is really built upon the love of God; whether we do "love him because he first loves us;" whether we are pure in heart: For this is the foundation which shall never be moved. "Blessed are the pure in heart: For they shall see God."[5]

Once again it is Kierkegaard who penetrates to the heart of the matter by saying that when the original second commandment is rightly understood, it can be converted logically into "Thou shalt love thyself in the right way." Only from loving oneself in the right way can one rightly love the neighbor. Thus they are analogous concepts.

> When the "as thyself" of the commandment has taken from you the selfishness which Christianity, sad to say, must presuppose as existing in every human being, then you have rightly learned to love yourself. Hence the law is: "You shall love yourself as you love your neighbor when you love him as you love yourself."[6]

In the most incisive fashion Kierkegaard then draws out some of the ethical implications of this interpretation that are worthy of being reproduced for consideration.

> When the busy man wastes his time and energy on vain and unimportant projects, is this not because he has not rightly learned to love himself? When the frivolous man abandons himself, almost as a mere nothing, to the folly of the moment, is not this because he does not rightly understand how to love himself? When the melancholy man wishes to be done with life, even with himself, is this not because he will not learn strictly and earnestly to love himself? When a man, because the world or another man faithlessly betrayed him, yields himself up to despair, how was he to blame (for we are not here

speaking of innocent suffering), except for not having loved himself in the right way? When a man in self-torment thinks to do God a service by torturing himself, what is his sin except this, of not willing to love himself in the right way? Ah, and when a man presumptuously lays his hand upon himself, does not his sin precisely consist in not loving himself in the way in which a man *ought* to love himself?[7]

Toward a Proper Self-Estimate

There are further ethical considerations to be noted. One aspect flows from the proper view of ourselves as servants of God. Socrates used this principle in a pagan context to argue against the legitimacy of suicide, one of the points made by Kierkegaard. In the Platonic dialogue that depicts the final hours of Socrates' life, he makes the puzzling assertion that the philosopher seeks death all his life. Someone suggests that this goal is easily achieved, but Socrates responds by the self-evident maxim that it is wrong to take another's property without his consent, and since we are the property of the gods, to deliberately end one's life prematurely is to do just this. Therefore our responsibility to our master prohibits it.

The Christian application of this principle is simple. As those who have been redeemed, we belong to the Lord. As Paul said, "You are not your own, you are bought with a price" (1 Cor 6:20; 7:23). Consequently we are called on to be good stewards of our bodies and minds and live for the glory of God.

This is highlighted by Paul in 1 Corinthians 6:19 as he speaks about the body being the temple of the Holy Spirit. Those who defile this temple will fall into divine disfavor. This principle has been the traditional support for many Christians' manifesting a long-standing opposition to the use of tobacco in any form. The recognition of its devastating effects on the human body only reinforces the basis for this stand. But the Christian uses this medical conclusion in a spiritual way. The person who is interested in health and long life may take seriously abstaining from tobacco products for just that reason, but Christians are different. They honor the Master to whom they belong, a distinctively theological rationale.

The same truth can be applied to other aspects of the care of the body, such as good diet. Obesity is not a sin, but gluttony certainly comes close. Gorging the body with food and drink that is detrimental to good health is not being a responsible steward.

We are also charged in Scripture with stewardship of the mind. Paul mentions this specifically in Philippians 1:10. His prayer is that the Philippians will learn to "discern what is best." This prayer is reinforced by his injunction in 4:8 to think about (meditate on) things that are true, noble, just, pure, lovely and admirable. In light of the diet fed to people today via the media, this principle has significant relevance.

Likewise, a proper relation to oneself calls for a healthy self-image. Much pop psychology speaks of the importance of self-esteem and often advises to assert oneself in order to achieve it. But from the Christian perspective recognizing oneself as a "child of the king" leaves no room for self-denigration or feelings of worthlessness. As an early TV commercial had a child say, "God don't make no junk."

PART IV

THE IMAGE OF GOD AS A BASIS FOR A SOCIAL ETHIC

Twelve

THE CHURCH
AND ETHICAL ACTION

Applying Christian ethics to society is difficult. On the one hand, there can be no Christian ethics without Christians, for Christian ethics is a response to the liberating grace of God. On the other hand, Christian ethics is a corollary of the theological understanding that we are made in the image of God. But in this sense all people are creatures of God, and if it is the highest fulfillment of human nature to actualize this *imago Dei*, then it would seem that an effort should be made to "impose" Christian ethical behavior on all people.

Two Inadequate Proposals
Two extreme approaches to this issue have emerged in the history of Christian thought. On the far right is *apocalypticism*, an attitude that has been present from the beginning of the Christian era—and before. On the left is a relatively recent phenomenon commonly termed the *social gospel*.

While *apocalypticism* has become a much-used term with a very technical (but difficult to define) meaning,[1] it is used here to reflect a particular attitude of pious people toward the world. Apocalypticism is pessimistic about society in general. It assumes that the present age is so corrupt that it is beyond redemption and must soon be brought to an end through divine judgment. Those who believe this way often withdraw into a kind of isolationism and make no effort to exert any influence on the world's institutions. Apocalypticism involves what can be called a lifeboat mentality. The ship is sinking, and only the few who flee the doomed vessel and seek safety in the lifeboat can be rescued. Nothing can be done to save the ship.

As scholars have pointed out, literature reflecting this kind of religious attitude has surfaced most widely during times that are hard for the righteous. It flowered during the mid-second century B.C. during the intense persecution of the Jews under Antiochus Epiphanes. It has been a widespread preoccupation during subsequent periods in Christian history when the impact of the church on society seemed inconsequential or the lot of the church became exceedingly difficult.

Scholars have pointed out the tension between apocalyptic theology and prophetic religion. The prophets of the Old Testament were "reformers," were more optimistic about the operation of God within history. Men like Amos, Hosea and Isaiah attacked the injustices of society and called on the people to bring the structures of society under the law of God and infuse them with justice and mercy. Of course, the bulk of their "reforming" was directed to the people of God. But a careful reading of these prophets reveals that they had an occasional word for Israel's neighbors that reflects a "creation ethic." In contrast, apocalypticism tended to abandon the world to the devil and to give it up as a lost cause.

The strength of apocalypticism is its recognition that the world order can never be equated with the kingdom of God, which can become a reality only through the activity of God. It can never emerge as a result of mere human activity. It takes very seriously the issue of sin in human life, acknowledging that all human ventures are eventually contaminated by sinfulness.

When taken to the extreme, the element in the Christian faith that leads to apocalypticism is what Winston L. King has called "inherent other-worldliness." While it may serve to inhibit the church's efforts to exert Christian influence in society, it does keep the church from losing its distinctive nature in the process.[2]

By contrast, the social gospel that emerged in the late nineteenth century and was prominent in the early twentieth century held out the hope that the kingdom of God could be brought about by Christianizing the social order. Unlike the traditional doctrine of sin, this philosophy maintained that the institutions of society were the bearers of original sin. People were what they were because of the influence of these forces on them. The consequence of such thinking was the view that if the social order could be reformed to reflect Christian values, the ills of humanity could be remedied and the golden age would be ushered in.

It is easy to see how personal conversion became of little importance and efforts were focused instead on redeeming the world through social action. Today such a view seems like an untenable rosy optimism that is completely naive concerning the depths of human depravity. But during certain times, like the period in which it flourished, when the world appeared to be making unprecedented progress with utopia just around the corner, it became easy to lapse into this kind of unrealistic thinking.

A Wesleyan View of the Christian in Society

Christian social ethics, viewed from a Wesleyan perspective, demand that both these extremes need to be avoided. Exerting Christian influence in the world is the God-given responsibility of all who would be the light of the world or the salt of the earth. What else can these metaphors mean? One can neither withdraw into isolationism nor accept the easy optimism that any society, whatever the government or economic system, can ever become completely Christian because of the fallen nature of humanity.

In expounding the metaphors of salt and light in the Sermon on the Mount, Wesley sets forth the premise based on their implications that "Christianity is essentially a social religion; and that to turn it into a solitary religion, is indeed to destroy it." On this basis he explicitly rejects the possibility of isolationism. In fact, he argues, if we choose this radical path of separation "we cannot be Christians at all."[3]

This question must now be considered: How does one exert Christian influence? Here again we encounter different perspectives. The conservative takes the position that if the social order is influenced in a Christianly way, it is through individual conversion. This is to say, one does not attempt to directly address unjust practices or corruption but rather seeks to bring people to Christ personally and by doing so changes the complexion of society.

On the surface, this position appears to have the support of Jesus and Paul. One can point to the apparent fact that neither of them forthrightly attacked any of the evil social institutions of their day, such as slavery. In fact, many passages, such as Paul's instructions to slaves in Ephesians 6:5-9, appear to condone slavery, at least implicitly. But some argue that Paul's letter to Philemon illustrates the way such matters should be addressed. He sent Onesimus, a runaway slave, back to his owner, Philemon, with the admonition that since they were both Christians the slave should be received as a brother. But brotherhood and slavery are inimical. Implicitly, then, the seeds of dissolution were being planted. But the issue is not as simple as it appears. Apart from some great upheaval in society created by external forces, such as the American Civil War, overturning slavery in Paul's day would depend on the near universal conversion of slaveholders. And even that would be no guarantee, since many slaveholders in the South were "devout" Christians and used the Bible to defend slavery.

However, this instinct for personal conversion is sound. It ensures that the church will not capitulate to the temptation to become a political lobbying group. But it should not insulate the church from social action, and history demonstrates that it has not. Research has conclusively shown that the movement stemming from the Wesleyan revival, which could never be accused of losing the emphasis on personal religious experience, has been extremely active in addressing social problems and attempting to meliorate social ills.[4]

However, there is also considerable evidence that the multiplying of individual Christians has not either automatically or necessarily led to the elimination of social ills. Some years ago David H. C. Read called attention to the "notorious fact that the very considerable revival of personal religion evidenced in the United Stated since World War II through the increased membership in the Churches and unprecedented response to mass evangelism calling for personal decision, has coincided with an alarming increase in the crime rate and social evils of all kinds." He suggests that it is "as if we were being warned that a purely private interpretation of the Christian ethic is incapable of exerting a major influence on the moral health of a nation."[5] Albert T. Rasmussen concurs that "being kind and faithful in the family, or pleasant and generous among one's vocational associates, or a friendly next-door-neighbor does not add up to effective influence in organizational and political structures that make the policies that determine the patterns of our societies." The reason for this, he states, is that such decisions are made "in a very different way from those in simple primary relations."[6]

This position, agreed on by most contemporary Christian ethicists, has been forcefully brought to the attention of the modern world by the influential work of Reinhold Niebuhr. Taking seriously the fallen nature of humankind and the stubborn resistance of the evil structures in society, he has proposed a "Christian realism" that has had a major impact on ethical thinking and provided the philosophy behind the reform efforts of many of his students, notably Martin Luther King.

The question now becomes "How do we go about doing this?" The next chapter will lay a theological foundation for some tentative proposals that are consistent with Wesleyan theology.

Thirteen

CREATION ETHICS
AND THE IMAGE OF GOD

Ⅰn the biblical references to humanity's being made in the image of God, there is a duality that must be reconciled. Christian theologians have been nearly unanimous in recognizing this duality to imply that humanity, although fallen, is still in the image of God *in some sense*. Many contemporary interpreters take this to mean that this characteristic is definitive of human personhood. Wesleyan theology develops this aspect of the *imago* through the doctrine of prevenient grace.

The Image of God as Constituting the Personal
The implication of this teaching for ethics is that there is a structure that God has built into the nature of things. This structure informs both the world order and human nature. Thus there is a way of life that is fulfilling of human personhood. Conversely, if this inherent structure is violated, the result is destructive.

Historically many philosophers have discussed this characteristic of human existence under the topic of natural law. Americans live under a constitution that was developed in light of the natural-law theory of John Locke. It was traditionally believed that this "law" could be grasped by human reason, and positive law should be the codification of this higher law.[1] Consequently, to live rationally would be to live according to the nature of things. In more recent times philosophers have been hesitant to claim that reason is capable of such discovery, and many have denied the validity of the concept of natural law. Furthermore, one of the more telling criticisms of the traditional teaching about natural law is that it has been used to support the status quo, a critique that carries a great deal of truth.

Theologically, natural law has often been related to the concept of natural theology and generally has been in disrepute since the Barthian critique of liberalism in the early part of the twentieth century. However, there are signs that theologians are returning to a recognition of some such concept, even if conceived in new ways.

The implication of our analysis of the image of God is that there is not only an ethical ideal that is applicable to the people of God (what we have called redemption ethics), but also an ethic that is appropriate to human persons as personal beings. While the former is explicitly developed throughout Scripture, the latter is less obviously discussed, but it is present in certain important ways.

A Creation Ethic in Scripture

Is there evidence for such a creation ethic in Scripture? There are indications of some aspects of it in the creation account. The narrative not only implies that the nature of humanity is social, but it also states that in God's judgment it is not good for man to be alone (Gen 2:18). It suggests that the answer to this aloneness in its most intimate form is monogamy. Thus to violate this inborn nature results in a destruction of the human psyche. I once had a man in one of my classes who was a missionary to a polygamous culture. As we talked about this in class, he described the situation as likely resulting from economic necessity, but the wives were very unhappy in such a relationship. In a sense their personhood was violated by sharing a husband.

Two novels appeared in the 1960s that created quite a stir and resulted in considerable discussion. Both George Orwell's *1984* and Aldous Huxley's *Brave New World* were science fiction but purported to depict the shape of the future. The implications of Huxley's novel are far more germane to our discussion than Orwell's vision, which is obviously passé. In the "brave new world," science ruled. Any form of "religion" that remained was purely naturalistic. Literature and studies that are traditionally associated with the liberal arts, that is, those things that are uniquely human in nature, were anathema and carefully censored. Any expression of purpose for human existence was avoided. The traditional family was nonexistent, human fetuses were conceived in test tubes, and natural birth was looked on as obscene. There was no enduring commitment of male to female; in fact, a long-term sexual relation between two persons was considered unacceptable. As one character said of his occasional sexual partner, "She thinks of herself as meat."

The question that this picture brings to mind is, Can human beings continue to exist as humans in this kind of ethos? Whatever Huxley intended by this Marxist-dominated representation of the future, in light of the theological vision of biblical faith, the answer is no! One character in this novel ultimately becomes the focal point and reflects the end result of such a less-than-human way of life. He is referred to in the story as "the savage" and was an accident resulting from his mother's failure to protect herself with the prevailing method of birth control. He was an embarrassment to her and to the culture as he constantly longed for maternal love and family relationship and revolted against the indiscriminate sexual activities in which everyone was engaged. In the end he hanged himself because he could not cope with it. He, I believe, is a paradigm of the human race when it turns away from its divinely intended destiny.

A further evidence in the creation story of a natural structure is suggested by the institution of the sabbath day, based on God's own creativity. Initially it was designated as a day of rest, and worship was not specifically mentioned. There have been some studies that have demonstrated that work, unrelieved by a sabbath rest, tends to become wearisome and inefficient.

The prophet Amos prophesied judgment on non-Israelite nations based on a "covenant of brotherhood" which they had violated (Amos 1:9). The nations surrounding Israel had fallen under this condemnation, he said, and will be punished for their unusual cruelty in war and for enslaving conquered people. This suggests that apart from any special revelation there is a way of relating to other human beings that violates the created structure of human togetherness, and such behavior will come under divine judgment. When the fiery words of Amos are brought to bear on Judah and Israel, the basis for condemnation becomes the covenant of grace. They are censured for religious sins (2:4-8) based on both special revelation and a special relationship to God.

Wisdom Literature as a Creation Ethic

The central biblical source of the creation ethic is the wisdom literature of the Old Testament, especially Proverbs. The wisdom books (Proverbs, Ecclesiastes, Song of Songs and Job) develop the concept of wisdom in different ways, some positive and some skeptical (as Ecclesiastes and Job), and raise some very interesting problems that unfortunately cannot be examined here. (There are many excellent sources for further study.[2])

This study will make general comments to highlight that this literature embodies a creation ethic. The central thesis of the Hebrew wisdom embodied in Proverbs and implied in the Song of Songs (which is a celebration of romantic love) is that God created the world and human nature according to a certain pattern. If humankind follows this pattern, life will be meaningful and successful. This is precisely how we have already defined natural law.

These structures can be discovered through experience. This is why the wise man is the one who is older and who has wide experience. Through this experience the wise man discovers what works and what does not. This wisdom is then passed on to the young and inexperienced.

If the young do not follow the advice of the elders, they are characterized as "fools."

One of the interesting supports for this view of wisdom is that "wisdom sayings" are found among all ancient peoples. Some of those sayings from Egyptian and other sources are incorporated among the proverbs of Israel. They are not given by special revelation but discovered by general experience.

Because wisdom for living is discovered by experience, it has a specific character. Proverbs, "short ethical sayings based on long experience," tell the reader how certain types of behavior normally or usually turn out. They do not declare that they will necessarily have the desired outcome. In this they are different from pronouncements based on a "thus saith the Lord." The proverb implicitly says, "Thus saith experience." For the scientifically minded this is similar to the probability of inductive logic.

The basic thesis of biblical wisdom is distinctively religious. Its fundamental premise is that "the fear of the LORD is the beginning of knowledge" (Prov 1:7). In other words, human nature is so created that life achieves full meaningfulness and true success only in a right relation to God. But beyond this there are numerous pieces of advice on how to simply get along in the world of people and things, the relationships that constitute the image of God. A reflection of all these relations is embedded ineradicably in human personhood, even though fallen.

The disadvantage of using Proverbs as the basis for a social ethic is that its teachings are chiefly individualistic, but even in that context some important insights can be gained. As we have already seen, the basic premise is religious: a right relation to God is the foundation of wisdom and wisdom's goal, the good life.

The early chapters of Proverbs, which mainly commend wisdom to the young, pose many warnings regarding improper sexual relations, with a prostitute (fornication) or with another's wife (adultery). The end result is both emotional and physical disease. Sexual diseases and especially

AIDS, which has assumed epidemic proportions in certain world areas, are grim illustrations of the validity of the wise man's advice.

In Proverbs 20:21 and 23:20-21 we find warnings against the undesirable consequences of strong drink (wine), namely violence and poverty. While it may not be possible to build a doctrine of abstinence on these passages—the only ones in the Bible that specifically speak to the issue—they certainly provide a basis for at least inferring such.

There is an ethic grounded in God's creative activity that relates to life in the world and pertains to all persons, whether redeemed or unredeemed. While it does have a theological basis, its presence can be recognized through experience, even when its theistic basis is undiscovered or unrecognized.

Creation and a Social Ethic

This aspect of the image as developed in a creation ethic is the basis for the Christian's social responsibility. Social ethics is a major concern of Christian ethicists, and rightly so. But what is it? One popular view sees social ethics exclusively in terms of doing good to those in need. It includes taking baskets of groceries to the poor at Thanksgiving and Christmas, providing shelters for the homeless, sending supplies to countries ravaged by natural disaster and so on. This is compassionate ministry and is a proper expression of the Christian spirit of love.

However, properly understood, social ethics includes the believer's involvement in attempting to do something about the structures of evil in society that produce the poverty, suffering and injustice in the world. This can sometimes be nasty and dangerous business, as many have discovered, because it often involves confronting society's powerful, who are resistant to being dislodged.

How does one go about this? Too many feel that the only way to address the evils in the world is by imposing a distinctive Christian ethic on society by law or other means. But Reinhold Niebuhr is quite realistic in saying that "it is impossible to construct a social ethic out of the ideal of love in its pure form, because the ideal presupposes the resolution of the conflict of life with life."[3] The virtual impossibility of imposing such an ethic on an alien temperament has caused many believers to withdraw from any effort to be redemptive and become isolationists.

But I suggest that a creation ethic serves as a sound basis for seeking to transform societal structures. It makes an appeal to humanity's self-interest, a motive to which even the unredeemed can relate. Christian evaluations of such matters as being "of the devil" or "sinful" will have little interest to the secular mind. But pointing out the destructive consequences for human life, happiness and dignity may likely make a greater impact.

Wesley's Social Ethic

A review of Wesley's personal approach to public issues in his own day reflects several stages of action, most of which assume a privileged position on his part as well as a better-than-average knowledge of the matters under consideration. In using Wesley's method as a guideline, one must keep in mind that he lived under a monarchy, and that gave a specific shape to some of his advice.

First of all, Wesley pointed out the advantage of the fear of God and the beneficence that would be bestowed by divine providence if one would follow God's law. Doubtless he knew that this was the most certain way of achieving a peaceful and just society. But realizing the need for other measures, he often pointed to the civil consequences of certain policies and practices. On one occasion he wrote a letter to the mayor and corporation of Bristol, voicing his objection to the establishment of a playhouse in the city. Although he avers that "most of the present stage entertainment saps the foundation of all religion as they naturally tend to efface all traces of piety and seriousness out of the minds of men," his major objection was based on his opinion that they

are peculiarly hurtful to a trading city, giving a wrong turn to youth especially, gay, trifling, and directly opposite to the spirit of industry and close application to business; and as drinking and debauchery of every kind are close attendants on these entertainments, with indolence, effeminacy, and idleness, which affect trade in a high degree.[4]

In discussing a critical shortage of food in England, Wesley addressed the issue in a manner similar to the way some contemporary prophets, such as Tom Sine and Ronald J. Sider, speak to a similar widespread hunger. Wesley's rationale has a double-barreled implication. He demonstrates that if the amount of grain used by distillers were channeled into food, and something were done about the economic impact on cattle farming of massive horse rearing purely to feed the vanity of the rich, the cost of food would be dramatically lowered and the supply would be sufficient for all to be adequately fed. But this incisive analysis was accompanied by a high degree of pessimism that anything would really be done, "for what good can we expect (suppose the Scriptures are true) for such a nation as this where there is no fear of God?"[5]

Much of his appeal for the alleviation of social ills is based on reason and the inherent worth of human persons. These are not "naturalistic" value judgments, however. They are based on what Wesley, in principle, refers to as the "law of nature," which was built into the structure of humanity by creative fiat. It is, as he says, "unchangeable reason; it is unalterable rectitude, it is the everlasting fitness of all things that are or ever were created."[6]

Even though this law was disrupted by sin, "the law of God, the moral law, a concomitant of human nature, *first by creation* and *then by grace,* remains as the standard of human relations, prescribing what is right with regard to God, to ourselves, and to all of God's creatures."[7]

Wesley applies this principle to the human situation when he addresses the question of liberty.

Every man living, as man, has a right to this, as he is a rational creature. The Creator gave him this right when he endowed him with understanding. And every man must judge for himself, because every man must give an account . . . to God. Consequently, this is inseparable from humanity. And God never did give authority to any man, or number of men, to deprive any child of man thereof, under any cloud or pretence whatever.[8]

He likewise uses it to call into question civil laws that justify slavery.

But can law, human law, change the nature of things? Can it turn darkness into light, or evil into good? By no means. Not withstanding ten thousand laws, right is right, and wrong is wrong still. . . . So that I still ask, who can reconcile this treatment of the Negroes, first and last, with either mercy or justice? Slavery is utterly inconsistent with any degree of natural justice. Unlike ownership in sheep, no one should ever be born a slave. "Liberty is the right of every human creature, as soon as he breathes the vital air, and no human law can deprive him of that right which he derives from the law of nature." The slave is the brother of the slave owner or trader and should be respected as such.[9]

While we stop short of making specific suggestions regarding logistics in seeking to implement social change today, the Wesleyan perspective and practice provides a basis for "light[ing] a candle rather than cursing the darkness."

In fact, one of Wesley's shorter tracts is on the subject "How far is it the duty of a Christian Minister to preach against politics?" He affirms that the primary business of the minister is to "preach Jesus Christ and him crucified," but allows that addressing public issues (in Wesley's case, defending the king against false calumnies) can be done infrequently "when fit occasion offers."[10]

Redemption ethics is not an arbitrary imposition of rules on servile followers of Christ, but guidelines for a meaningful family life within the community of faith and the actualization of the *imago Dei,* the essence of human nature. Creation ethics is the basis for understanding how human society will survive and achieve a measure of justice in God's world with the hope that it will lead to the ultimate goal for which the Creator designed his most exalted creatures.

Notes

Chapter 1: Factors That Affect Moral Seriousness

[1]William Barclay, *Ethics in a Permissive Society* (New York: Harper & Row, 1971), p. 13.

[2]John Wesley, *The Works of John Wesley,* 3rd ed., 14 vols. (London: Wesleyan Methodist Book Room, 1872; reprint Kansas City, Mo.: Beacon Hill, 1978), 5:58. Hereafter, *Works.*

[3]Martin Luther, *Luther's Works,* ed. Jaroslav Pelikan, 55 vols. (St. Louis: Concordia, 1963), 26:231-33.

[4]*Works,* 7:204.

[5]Charles R. Swindoll, *The Grace Awakening* (Dallas: Word, 1990), p. 24. Emphasis added to highlight the unconditional relation being taught.

[6]Randy L. Maddox, *Responsible Grace* (Nashville: Kingswood, 1994).

[7]*Works,* 5:141. For an illuminating analysis of these two views of grace see Maddox, *Responsible Grace,* pp. 84-87.

[8]*Works,* 7:205.

[9]Albert Outler, "The Place of Wesley in the Christian Tradition," in *The Place of Wesley in the Christian Tradition,* ed. Kenneth Rowe (Metuchen, N.J.: Scarecrow, 1976); *Theology in the Wesleyan Spirit* (Nashville: Discipleship Resources-Tidings, 1975).

[10]Robert Bruce McLaren, *Christian Ethics* (Englewood Cliffs, N.J.: Prentice-Hall, 1994), p. 113. McLaren's argument is based on the superficial observation that the idea of "being born again" was addressed only to Nicodemus. This overlooks the fact that the concept of regeneration is a pervasive one throughout the New Testament. See, for example, 1 Peter 1:3, where "new birth" language is explicitly used.

[11]Cf. Paul Hessert, *The Christian Life,* New Directions in Theology Today 5 (Philadelphia: Westminster, 1967).

Chapter 2: The Need for a Theological Ethic

[1]John Stuart Mill, *Utilitarianism* (Indianapolis: Bobbs-Merrill, 1957), p. 28.

[2]Oswald Chambers, *The Philosophy of Sin* (London: Simpkin Marshall, 1941), p. 61. Wesleyan theology *does* hold that the formal aspect of conscience is attributed to the activity of prevenient grace.

[3]Quoted in Leon O. Hynson, *To Reform the Nation* (Grand Rapids, Mich.: Zondervan,

1984), p. 82.

[4]Immanuel Kant, *Critique of Pure Reason,* trans. Norman Kemp Smith (New York: St. Martin's, 1929), p. 93. Kant's verbatim phrase, using his own specialized jargon, was "Thoughts without content are empty, intuitions without concepts are blind."

[5]Christopher J. H. Wright, *An Eye for an Eye* (Downers Grove, Ill.: InterVarsity Press, 1983), pp. 176-77.

[6]McLaren, *Christian Ethics,* p. 75.

[7]Ibid., p. 97.

[8]Waldemar Janzen, *Old Testament Ethics: A Paradigmatic Approach* (Louisville: Westminster/John Knox, 1994), p. 17. Janzen's development of his thesis is quite different from the thesis I am proposing. He is suggesting that character stories embody paradigms that are not identical with the characters themselves and that these paradigms are nonconceptual and influence behavior by being internalized. Furthermore, they are not unchanged across time but are apparently always in flux. As a matter of fact, each story contributes some aspects to the developing paradigm. By contrast to my proposal, this characteristic seems to completely subjectivize and relativize ethical criteria. If we cannot define conceptually what a "good driver" (his example) is, then each person is left to determine his own "impression" of the paradigm of a "good driver" or "wise person" or "honest person," etc. This, I submit, will not do. A popular book that seeks to deal with the issue of how the Bible serves as a resource for Christian ethics is Bruce C. Birch and Larry L. Rasmussen, *Bible and Ethics in the Christian Life* (Minneapolis: Augsburg, 1989).

[9]John Bright, *The Authority of the Old Testament* (Grand Rapids, Mich.: Baker, 1975).

[10]Many recent biblical commentaries have begun to take seriously the theological content of Scripture and have by design gone beyond the typical grammatico-historical stage of exegesis. This makes them much more helpful than the older style, which seldom entered into this aspect of exegesis. See, for example, New International Theological Commentary on the Old Testament and New International Commentary on the Old Testament (Eerdmans), New International Commentary on the New Testament (Eerdmans), Westminster Bible Companion (Westminster) and numerous individual volumes.

[11]Cf. his sermon "The Lord Our Righteousness."

[12]Outler, *Theology in the Wesleyan Spirit,* p. 51.

[13]Augustine, *The Spirit and the Letter,* in *A Select Library of the Nicene and Post-Nicene Fathers of the Christian Church,* ed. Philip Schaff, 14 vols. (Grand Rapids, Mich.: Eerdmans, 1956), 5:83-114. See especially chap. 47.

[14]For a full discussion that includes a comparison of the two traditions, see Alister E. McGrath, *Christian Theology: An Introduction* (Oxford: Blackwell, 1994), pp. 381-92.

[15]*Works,* 5:56-57.

[16]Ibid., p. 57.

[17]Bernhard Anderson, *Out of the Depths* (Philadelphia: Westminster 1983), pp. 100-101.

[18]Gustaf Aulén, *Christus Victor,* trans. A. G. Herbert (New York: Macmillan, 1961), p. 92.

[19]Recent Wesley studies have become more aware of the influence of Eastern Orthodox thought on Wesley's views. This insight, like many others, was pioneered by Albert Outler.

Chapter 3: Important Concepts for Ethical Refection

[1]See H. Ray Dunning, *Grace, Faith and Holiness* (Kansas City, Mo.: Beacon Hill, 1988), pp. 59-60, for a full-scale analysis of this truth.

[2]David Hume, *A Treatise of Human Nature* (Oxford: Clarendon, 1987), pp. 413-18.

[3]John Wesley, *A Plain Account of Christian Perfection* (Kansas City, Mo.: Beacon Hill, 1968), p. 42.

[4]See pp. 33-36 for a full explanation of the technical terms *teleological* and *deontological.*

[5]Perhaps the most obvious example of this approach is the French atheistic existentialist Jean-Paul Sartre. In his essay "Existentialism Is a Humanism" he denies both that God exists and that there is a "human nature." Thus each individual must choose him- or herself, that is, create his or her own values with no objective guidance whatsoever.

[6]Quoted without reference in Samuel E. Stumpf, *Philosophy: History and Problems* (New York: McGraw-Hill, 1971), pp. 475-76.

[7]See H. Ray Dunning, "Ethics in a Wesleyan Context," *Wesleyan Theological Journal* 5, no. 1 (Spring 1970).

[8]Cf. R. Newton Flew, *The Idea of Perfection in Christian Theology* (London: Oxford University Press, 1934).

[9]Albert Outler, *Theology in the Wesleyan Spirit* (Nashville: Discipleship Resources-Tidings, 1975), p. 81. Even though Wesley primarily used the term "Christian perfection" as synonymous with "entire sanctification" and spoke of it as a present possibility in this life, he was always careful to speak of the Christian journey in dynamic terms, stressing the lifelong maturation in pursuit of the image of God. Thus Outler's judgment is undoubtedly applicable to Wesley's views.

[10]Ibid.

[11]See H. Ray Dunning, "Nazarene Ethics As Seen in a Theological, Historical and Sociological Context," Ph.D. dissertation, Vanderbilt University, 1969.

[12]That this perception was widespread is indicated by the fact that in 1976 the Church of the Nazarene added a paragraph to its Articles of Faith emphasizing the lifelong maturation of the Christian life in an obvious attempt to counter this misunderstanding.

[13]C. Harald Lindström, *Wesley and Sanctification: A Study in the Doctrine of Salvation* (Wilmore, Ky.: Francis Asbury, n.d.).

[14]See Dunning, "Nazarene Ethics."

[15]I am indebted to Albert Outler for the terms *perfected* and *perfectible* perfection.

[16]Sermon on "Christian Perfection," in *Standard Sermons of John Wesley,* ed. E. H. Sugden, 2 vols. (London: Epworth, 1964), 2:156.

[17]Outler, *Theology in the Wesleyan Spirit,* p. 81.

[18]*Works,* 5:80.

[19]Ibid., 6:243.

[20]Ibid., p. 272.

Chapter 4: Image of God

[1]Philip Edgecombe Hughes, *The True Image* (Grand Rapids, Mich.: Eerdmans, 1989), p. 49.

[2]See Paul M. Bassett and William M. Greathouse, *The Historical Development,* vol. 2 of *Exploring Christian Holiness* (Kansas City, Mo.: Beacon Hill, 1985). The section by Bassett carefully demonstrates the teaching of many of the church fathers that "entire sanctification" is a possibility in this life, thus showing it to be an uninterrupted belief through the entire first seventeen centuries A.D.

[3]Quoted in Thomas Cook, *New Testament Holiness* (London: Epworth, 1950), p. 43.

[4]Paul Ramsey, *Basic Christian Ethics* (New York: Scribner's, 1950), p. 252.

[5]Dietrich Bonhoeffer, *Creation and Fall* (London: SCM Press, 1962); Douglas John Hall, *Imaging God* (Grand Rapids, Mich.: Eerdmans, 1986); Arthur F. Holmes, *Contours of a World View* (Grand Rapids, Mich.: Eerdmans, 1983), pp. 107-26; Ray S. Anderson, *On Being Human* (Grand Rapids, Mich.: Eerdmans, 1982); Ramsey, *Basic Christian Ethics.*

[6]J. N. D. Kelly, *Early Christian Doctrines* (San Francisco: Harper & Row, 1978), p. 275.

[7]H. Orton Wiley, *Christian Theology,* 3 vols. (Kansas City, Mo.: Beacon Hill, 1946), pp. 7-79. Wiley, an influential theologian in the Wesleyan tradition from an earlier generation, interpreted Christian ethics almost exclusively in terms of obligation. This is consistent with a mainstream emphasis of the American Holiness movement that sanctification functions to remove the rebellion within the human heart, resulting in a spirit of obedience to law. Wiley has some valuable insights and helpful discussions, but they are set in the context of law and duty. There is no evidence of any other ethical principle, and thus he draws some of his observations about duties from other than "revealed sources," for instance, John Locke's philosophy about natural law (pp. 74-76).

[8]Christopher J. H. Wright, *An Eye for an Eye* (Downers Grove, Ill.: InterVarsity Press, 1983), pp. 19-20.

[9]Bonhoeffer, *Creation and Fall,* p. 37.

[10]Hall, *Imaging God,* p. 55.

[11]Elmer Martens, *God's Design* (Grand Rapids, Mich.: Baker, 1981), p. 28.

[12]Holmes, *Contours of a World View,* p. 113.

[13]In German folklore, on the eve of May Day, or the feast of St. Walpurgis, a witches' sabbath took place on a peak in the Hartz Mountains. This was known as Walpurgis Night.

[14]Bonhoeffer, *Creation and Fall,* p. 38.

[15]Irenaeus took these two terms in Genesis 1:26, *image* and *likeness,* to refer to different realities rather than recognizing it as a Hebrew parallelism. He interpreted *image* as referring to humanity's nature as rational and free, a nature not lost at the Fall. *Likeness* refers to a supernatural gift of God that should be understood as spiritual and probably ethical in nature. This was lost at the Fall. As developed in Western theology and articulated by Thomas Aquinas, these two reflected the juxtaposition of nature and grace, the latter being an added gift imposed on a good nature so that humankind's natural end and supernatural end might be achieved. Irenaeus's own interpretation set the pattern for subsequent Eastern Orthodoxy, which taught that the likeness was present in germ, awaiting maturation. That is, Adam and Even were created innocent but not perfect. This became in Eastern thought the basis for a dynamic understanding of the Christian life that profoundly influenced John Wesley's doctrine of sanctification. For a fuller discussion of Irenaeus's teaching see David Cairns, *The Image of God in Man* (New York: Philosophical Library, 1953), pp. 73-83. For the influence of these ideas on Wesley see Randy Maddox, *Responsible Grace* (Nashville: Kingswood, 1994), pp. 65-67.

[16]John Macmurray, *Persons in Relation* (London: Faber & Faber, 1961).

[17]Anthony Campolo, *A Reasonable Faith* (Waco, Tex: Word, 1983), p. 160.

[18]Anderson, *On Being Human,* pp. 6-8.

Chapter 5: Salvation as Restoration

[1]Quoted by E. F. Kevan, "Genesis," in *New Bible Commentary,* ed. F. Davidson, 2nd ed. (Grand Rapids, Mich.: Eerdmans, 1960).

[2]John Wesley, "The Righteousness of Faith," in *Standard Sermons of John Wesley,* ed. E. H. Sugden, 2 vols. (London: Epworth, 1964), 1:143.

[3]*Works,* 6:276. See also p. 509.

[4]Ibid., 10:229-30.

[5]Ibid., 6:512. Wesley himself consistently used the term *preventing grace,* but this is the same as *prevenient* grace.

[6]Harald Lindström, *Wesley and Sanctification* (Wilmore, Ky.: Francis Asbury, n.d.), p. 45.

[7]For a clear and consistent articulation of this view, see R. C. Sproul, *The Mystery of the Holy Spirit* (Wheaton, Ill.: Tyndale, 1990).

[8]Lindström, *Wesley and Sanctification,* p. 42.

[9]Mildred Bangs Wynkoop, *A Theology of Love* (Kansas City, Mo.: Beacon Hill, 1972).

[10]*Works,* 6:488.

[11]Ibid., p. 489.

Chapter 6: Christian Ethics

[1]Arnold B. Rhodes, *The Mighty Acts of God* (Richmond, Va.: CLC Press, 1964), p. 80.

[2]George Eldon Ladd, *A Theology of the New Testament* (Grand Rapids, Mich.: Eerdmans, 1974), p. 67.

[3]George Hunter III, dean of the E. Stanley Jones School of Evangelism at Asbury Theological Seminary, in a sermon in the chapel of Trevecca Nazarene University, made a compelling case, based on the story of the demoniac found in Matthew 8:28-34, that the contemporary form of demon possession is addiction.

[4]Christopher J. H. Wright, *An Eye for an Eye* (Downers Grove, Ill.: InterVarsity Press, 1983), p. 22.

[5]Oswald Chambers, *The Highest Good* (London: Simpkin Marshall, 1941), p. 16.

[6]Robert Chiles, *Theological Transition in American Methodism* (New York: Abingdon, 1965), p. 16.

[7]Lawrence E. Toombs, "Love and Justice in Deuteronomy: A Third Approach to the Law," *Interpretation* 19 (1965): 400.

[8]Ibid., p. 401.

[9]Ibid.

[10]*Works,* 5:303-4.

[11]Ibid., 3:328.

[12]Ibid., 5:267. Notice the similarity to the Neo-Platonic pattern of Augustine's thought. It is very much like his "Thou hast made us for thyself, and our hearts are restless until they rest in Thee," as stated in the opening of Augustine's *Confessions.*

[13]See Adolf von Harnack, *The Essence of Christianity* (New York: Harper, 1957).

[14]Chambers, *Highest Good,* pp. 14-15.

[15]John Wesley, *Standard Sermons of John Wesley,* ed. E. H. Sugden, 2 vols. (London: Epworth, 1964), 2:50.

[16]One of the earliest theologians to argue this point was Irenaeus, who lived in the second century. In many ways Irenaeus anticipated the views of John Wesley in the eighteenth century.

[17]*Works,* 5:436. This statement and its implications are not invalidated by Wesley's teaching about a "covenant of works" that was borrowed from Federal Calvinism and which E. H. Sugden properly criticizes as being a fiction without foundation. Here is another case of Wesley using a prevailing theological concept uncritically

since it does not fit in with his central commitments.

[18]Campolo, *Reasonable Faith*, pp. 162-63.

[19]Theodorus C. Vriezen, *An Outline of Old Testament Theology* (Wageningen, Holland: H. Veenman and Zonen, 1958), p. 167.

[20]Wright, *An Eye for an Eye*, p. 41.

Chapter 7: The Image as Relation to God

[1]*Works*, 6:489.

[2]John Wesley, *Standard Sermons of John Wesley*, ed. E. H. Sugden, 2 vols. (London: Epworth, 1964), 1:151.

[3]Ibid.

[4]Ibid., pp. 153-55.

[5]Ibid., p. 327. See also p. 342.

[6]Gene Outka, *Agape: An Ethical Analysis* (New Haven, Conn.: Yale University Press, 1972), p. 46.

[7]From Søren Kierkegaard, "Works of Love," in *A Kierkegaard Anthology*, ed. Robert Bretall (New York: Modern Library, 1946), p. 286.

[8]Susannah Wesley, quoted in *The Works of John Wesley*, ed. Frank Baker, 25 vols. (Oxford: Clarendon, 1980), 25:166.

[9]Cf. H. Ray Dunning, "Nazarene Ethics As Seen in a Theological, Historical and Sociological Context," Ph.D. dissertation, Vanderbilt University, 1969.

[10]Several good Old Testament scholars have advocated this position, but Gordon Wenham cautions against this being the total explanation. See Gordon J. Wenham, *The Book of Leviticus*, New International Commentary on the Old Testament (Grand Rapids, Mich.: Eerdmans, 1979).

Chapter 8: The Image as Relation to Others

[1]This does mean that the New Testament revelation of God as threefold in nature is not in contradiction with Hebrew monotheism.

[2]Philip Edgecombe Hughes, *The True Image* (Grand Rapids, Mich.: Eerdmans, 1989), p. 52.

[3]These statements are obviously derived from my own experience and may not reflect the experience of others. Hence I do not set them out as universally true dogma.

[4]Victor Paul Furnish, *The Love Command in the New Testament* (Nashville: Abingdon, 1972), pp. 46-53.

[5]Gustaf Aulén, *Jesus in Contemporary Historical Research* (Philadelphia: Fortress, 1976), p. 138.

[6]Paul Ramsey, *Basic Christian Ethics* (New York: Scribner's, 1950), p. 101.

[7]Furnish, *Love Command*, p. 50.

[8]Ibid., p. 45.

[9]William Barclay, *New Testament Words* (Philadelphia: Westminster, 1974), pp. 17-29.

[10]Søren Kierkegaard, "Works of Love," in *A Kierkegaard Anthology,* ed. Robert Bretall (New York: Modern Library, 1946), pp. 295-96.

[11]Ibid., pp. 286-87.

[12]"The Use of Money," *Works,* 6:24-25.

[13]H. Orton Wiley, *Christian Theology,* 3 vols. (Kansas City, Mo.: Beacon Hill, 1946), 3:50.

Chapter 9: The Church as Context for Christian Ethics

[1]Cf. George L. Hunt, *Rediscovering the Church* (New York: Association Press, 1956); William Robinson, *The Biblical Doctrine of the Church* (St. Louis: Bethany Press, 1960).

[2]David H. C. Read, *Christian Ethics* (Philadelphia: J. B. Lippincott, 1968), p. 66.

[3]Gordon D. Kaufman, *The Context of Decision* (New York: Abingdon, 1961), p. 28.

[4]Cf. R. Newton Flew, *Jesus and His Church* (London: Epworth, 1938); Joseph B. Clower Jr., *The Church in the Thought of Jesus* (Richmond, Va.: John Knox, 1959).

[5]This is the way extreme forms of fundamentalism, as well as "folk literalism," interprets the concept of revelation, refusing to acknowledge the historically and culturally conditioned aspect of what has been "revealed."

[6]Paul Tillich, *Systematic Theology,* 3 vols. (New York: Harper & Row, 1967), 1:148. Emphasis added.

[7]A. T. Rasmussen, *Christian Social Ethics* (Englewood Cliffs, N.J.: Prentice-Hall, 1956), p. 24.

[8]Ibid., pp. 10-11.

Chapter 10: The Image as Relation to the Earth

[1]Patrick D. Miller Jr., "The Gift of Land," *Interpretation* 23, no. 4 (October 1969): 462.

[2]For an excellent discussion of the absence of the land from New Testament theology see Christopher J. H. Wright, *An Eye for an Eye* (Downers Grove, Ill.: InterVarsity Press, 1983), pp. 92-102, which comes to a somewhat different, though not antithetical, conclusion.

[3]Oswald Chambers, *The Highest Good* (London: Simpkin Marshall, 1941), p. 23.

[4]Miller, "Gift of Land," p. 464.

[5]*Works,* 5:374.

[6]Ibid., 6:124-36.

[7]Ibid., 5:367.

[8]Ibid., 7:9.

[9]Ibid., p. 10.

Chapter 11: The Image as Relation to Self

[1]Paul Ramsey, *Basic Christian Ethics* (New York: Scribner's, 1950), p. 101.

[2]From *Philosophical Fragments,* quoted in Ramsey, *Basic Christian Ethics,* p. 101, n. 8. Emphasis added by Ramsey.

[3]*Works,* 5:263.

[4]George F. Thomas, *Christian Ethics and Moral Philosophy* (New York: Charles Scribner's Sons, 1955), p. 57.

[5]*Works,* 5:278.

[6]Søren Kierkegaard, in *A Kierkegaard Anthology,* ed. Robert Bretall (New York: Modern Library, 1946), p. 289.

[7]Ibid., pp. 289-90.

Chapter 12: The Church and Ethical Action

[1]See Leon Morris, *Apocalyptic* (Grand Rapids, Mich.: Eerdmans, 1972).

[2]Winston L. King, *The Holy Imperative* (New York: Harper, 1949), p. 180.

[3]*Works,* 5:296-99.

[4]Timothy L. Smith, *Revivalism and Social Reform* (Nashville: Abingdon, 1957); Donald Dayton, *Discovering an Evangelical Heritage* (New York: Harper & Row, 1976).

[5]David H. C. Read, *Christian Ethics* (Philadelphia: J. B. Lippincott, 1968), p. 68.

[6]A. T. Rasmussen, *Christian Social Ethics* (Englewood Cliffs, N.J.: Prentice-Hall, 1956), pp. 7-8.

Chapter 13: Creation Ethics and the Image of God

[1]The classic exposition of this theory is found in Thomas Aquinas.

[2]For example, R. B. Y. Scott, *The Way of Wisdom in the Old Testament* (New York: Collier, 1986); R. B. Y. Scott, *Proverbs and Ecclesiastes,* Anchor Bible 18 (Garden City, N.Y.: Doubleday, 1965).

[3]Quoted in Gene Outka, *Agape: An Ethical Analysis* (New Haven, Conn.: Yale University Press, 1972), p. 26.

[4]*Works,* 12:128.

[5]Ibid., "Thoughts on the Present Scarcity of Provisions," 11:53-59.

[6]John Wesley, *Standard Sermons of John Wesley,* ed. E. H. Sugden, 2 vols. (London: Epworth, 1964), 2:41-47.

[7]Leon O. Hynson, *To Reform the Nation* (Grand Rapids, Mich.: Zondervan, 1984), p. 73. Note the complex of relations that we have identified as constituting the *imago Dei.*

[8]*Works,* 11:157.

[9]Ibid., 8:13.

[10]Ibid., 11:154-55.

Bibliography

Anderson, Bernhard. *Out of the Depths*. Philadelphia: Westminster, 1983.

Anderson, Ray S. *On Being Human*. Grand Rapids, Mich.: Eerdmans, 1982.

Aulén, Gustaf. *Christus Victor*. Trans. A. G. Herbert. New York: Macmillan, 1961.

———. *Jesus in Contemporary Historical Research*. Philadelphia: Fortress, 1976.

Barclay, William. *Ethics in a Permissive Society*. New York: Harper & Row, 1971.

Bassett, Paul M., and William M. Greathouse. *Exploring Christian Holiness*. Vol. 2, *The Historical Development*. Kansas City, Mo.: Beacon Hill, 1985.

Bonhoeffer, Dietrich. *Creation and Fall*. London: SCM Press, 1962.

Bright, John. *The Authority of the Old Testament*. Grand Rapids, Mich.: Baker, 1975.

Campolo, Anthony. *A Reasonable Faith*. Waco, Tex.: Word, 1983.

Chambers, Oswald. *The Highest Good*. London: Simpkin Marshall, 1941.

———. *The Philosophy of Sin*. London: Simpkin Marshall, 1941.

Chiles, Robert. *Theological Transition in American Methodism*. New York: Abingdon, 1965.

Clower, Joseph B., Jr. *The Church in the Thought of Jesus*. Richmond, Va.: John Knox, 1959.

Cook, Thomas. *New Testament Holiness*. London: Epworth, 1950.

Dunning, H. Ray. "Ethics in a Wesleyan Context." *Wesleyan Theological Journal* 5, no. 1 (Spring 1970).

———. *Grace, Faith and Holiness*. Kansas City, Mo.: Beacon Hill, 1988.

———. "Nazarene Ethics As Seen in a Theological, Historical and Sociological Context." Ph.D. dissertation, Vanderbilt University, 1969.

Flew, R. Newton. *The Idea of Perfection in Christian Theology*. London: Oxford University Press, 1934.

———. *Jesus and His Church*. London: Epworth, 1938.

Furnish, Victor Paul. *The Love Command in the New Testament*. Nashville: Abingdon, 1972.

Hall, Douglas John. *Imaging God*. Grand Rapids, Mich.: Eerdmans, 1986.

Harnack, Adolf von. *The Essence of Christianity*. New York: Harper, 1957.

Hessert, Paul. *New Directions in Theology Today*. Vol. 5, *The Christian Life*. Philadelphia: Westminster, 1967.

Holmes, Arthur F. *Contours of a World View*. Grand Rapids, Mich.: Eerdmans, 1983

Hughes, Philip E. *The True Image.* Grand Rapids, Mich.: Eerdmans, 1989.

Hunt, George L. *Rediscovering the Church.* New York: Association Press, 1956.

Hynson, Leon O. *To Reform the Nation.* Grand Rapids, Mich.: Zondervan, 1984.

Janzen, Waldemar. *Old Testament Ethics: A Paradigmatic Approach.* Louisville, Ky.: Westminster/John Knox, 1994.

Kaufman, Gordon D. *The Context of Decision.* New York: Abingdon, 1961.

Kelly, J. N. D. *Early Christian Doctrines.* San Francisco: Harper & Row, 1978.

Kevan, E. F. "Genesis." In *New Bible Commentary.* Ed. F. Davidson. 2nd ed. Grand Rapids, Mich.: Eerdmans, 1960.

Kierkegaard, Søren. *A Kierkegaard Anthology.* Ed. Robert Bretall. New York: Modern Library, 1946.

Ladd, George Eldon. *A Theology of the New Testament.* Grand Rapids, Mich.: Eerdmans, 1974.

Lindström, C. Harald. *Wesley and Sanctification: A Study in the Doctrine of Salvation.* Wilmore, Ky.: Francis Asbury, n.d.

Macmurray, John. *Persons in Relation.* London: Faber & Faber, 1961.

Maddox, Randy L. *Responsible Grace.* Nashville: Kingswood, 1994.

Martens, Elmer. *God's Design.* Grand Rapids, Mich.: Baker, 1981.

McLaren, Robert Bruce. *Christian Ethics.* Englewood Cliffs, N.J.: Prentice-Hall, 1994.

Mill, John Stuart. *Utilitarianism.* Indianapolis: Bobbs-Merrill, 1957.

Miller, Patrick D. "The Gift of Land." *Interpretation* 23, no. 4 (October 1969).

Outka, Gene. *Agape: An Ethical Analysis.* New Haven, Conn.: Yale University Press, 1972.

Outler, Albert. "The Place of Wesley in the Christian Tradition." In *The Place of Wesley in the Christian Tradition.* Ed. Kenneth Rowe. Metuchen, N.J.: Scarecrow, 1976.

————. *Theology in the Wesleyan Spirit.* Nashville: Discipleship Resources-Tidings, 1975

Ramsey, Paul. *Basic Christian Ethics.* New York: Charles Scribner's Sons, 1950.

Rasmussen, A. T. *Christian Social Ethics.* Englewood Cliffs, N.J.: Prentice-Hall, 1956.

Read, David H. C. *Christian Ethics.* Philadelphia: J. B. Lippincott, 1968.

Rhodes, Arnold B. *The Mighty Acts of God.* Richmond, Va.: CLC Press, 1964.

Robinson, William. *The Biblical Doctrine of the Church.* St. Louis: Bethany, 1960.

Sproul, R. C. *The Mystery of the Holy Spirit.* Wheaton, Ill.: Tyndale, 1990.

Swindoll, Charles R. *The Grace Awakening.* Dallas: Word, 1990.

Tillich, Paul. *Systematic Theology.* 3 vols. New York: Harper & Row, 1967.

Toombs, Lawrence E. "Love and Justice in Deuteronomy: A Third Approach to the Law." *Interpretation* 19 (1965).

Vriezen, Theodorus C. *An Outline of Old Testament Theology.* Wageningen,

Holland: H. Veenman and Zonen, 1958.

Wenham, Gordon J. *The Book of Leviticus*. New International Commentary on the Old Testament. Grand Rapids, Mich.: Eerdmans, 1979.

Wesley, John. *A Plain Account of Christian Perfection*. Kansas City, Mo.: Beacon Hill, 1968.

————. *Standard Sermons of John Wesley*. Ed. E. H. Sugden. 2 vols. London: Epworth, 1964.

————. *The Works of John Wesley*. 3rd ed. 14 vols. London: Wesleyan Methodist Book Room, 1872; reprint Kansas City, Mo.: Beacon Hill, 1978.

Wiley, H. Orton. *Christian Theology*. 3 vols. Kansas City, Mo.: Beacon Hill, 1946.

Wright, Christopher J. H. *An Eye for an Eye*. Downers Grove, Ill.: InterVarsity Press, 1983.

Wynkoop, Mildred Bangs. *A Theology of Love*. Kansas City, Mo.: Beacon Hill, 1972.

Subject and Person Index

Scripture Index